MODERN UPHOLSTERING TECHNIQUES

MODERN UPHOLSTERING TECHNIQUES

Robert J McDonald

Charles Scribner's Sons
New York

1 3 5 7 9 11 13 15 17 19 I/C 20 18 16 14 12 10 8 6 4 2

Printed in Great Britain
ISBN 0-684-16837-5
Library of Congress Catalog Number: 80-54577

4

Contents

Acknowledgment

The author acknowledges with gratitude the material and photographs supplied by the following organisations: Pirelli Ltd; Senco Pneumatics (UK) Ltd; Du Pont (UK) Ltd; Dunlop Semtex Ltd, Industrial Products Division; Dunlop Ltd, Dunlopillo Division; Fisco Products Ltd; Profile Expanded Plastics Ltd.

The colour plate on the front jacket is by Dennis Gasser, LCF, and the chair on the back jacket was designed by Theo Hopkins, LCF.

Introduction

This book was written in response to encouragement from the upholstery trade, the publisher and friends following the widespread interest in my previous book, *Upholstery Repair and Restoration,* which was first published in 1977 and is currently in its second impression. With the knowledge that my first effort was not in vain, I have put pen to paper once again to cover a particular aspect of upholstery in more detail, and trust that it will help students and amateurs to understand and enjoy this thoroughly rewarding craft.

I started work at the age of 14, serving a six-year apprenticeship with a reputable upholstery firm, and was a journeyman with a substantial background in craft training when the Second World War involved me in military service. Enlisting in a transport company, I then spent six years on active service in North Africa and Italy, managing nevertheless to find ways of 'keeping my hand in', and practising the skilful art of creating comfort with my hands.

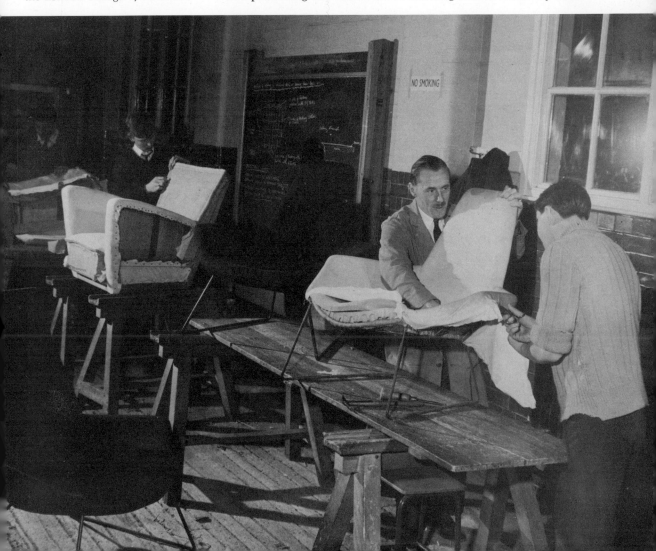

1 The author conducting a class at the London College of Furniture

My return to the upholstery trade after the war saw a change in the nature of my work. It was not long before I found myself working on the upholstery cover cutting bench and controlling production of the upholstery workshop. A further opportunity came about in the form of a part-time teaching post at the London College of Furniture and after two years I was invited to accept a full-time post there. Now, after more than 20 years spent teaching the craft, while at the same time keeping close links with contemporary design in industry, I feel well qualified to write on the various aspects of modern upholstery work.

It is a fact that professional upholsterers tend to specialise in a particular field, as a result of intense early training. Thus a craftsman skilled in traditional work or restoration may not venture to cope with modern designs and materials, and vice versa. This is unfortunate, as it has always been my contention that an upholsterer worth his salt should be capable of undertaking any type of upholstery, and students should be trained in all aspects of traditional and contemporary work.

I hope this book will provide concise information and clear instruction to meet the needs of the student, and the home upholsterer interested in the serious aspect of the craft, and explain how to achieve the most professional results for all types of modern furniture.

Developments in Modern Upholstery

Upholstery was once classed as one of the élite crafts, and the upholsterer was highly respected by other so-called 'common' craftsmen. He was expected to be capable of undertaking not only furniture upholstery but also curtains and drapes, wall coverings, floor coverings and mattress making, and might even be called upon to upholster the interior of a coffin: indeed his title 'upholsterer' derived from that of the 'upholder' of household furnishings. Today, of course, these crafts have become separate specialist trades with their own well defined boundaries.

Throughout the years changes in furniture styles and designs have been brought about by changing conditions, developments in tools and machinery, the introduction of new materials and the socio-economic conditions of the time.

The introduction of mass production methods into upholstery in an attempt to speed up production, keep costs low, and reduce the high skill and labour content of the work, was first seen in 1904, when a 'spring assembly' patented by W E Morris was developed as the first labour-savour device, and became the forerunner of the spring unit which is still in use in deeply sprung seats today.

The 'pocketed' spring was developed by the Vi-spring company during the 1920s and 1930s. These springs were cylindrical, about 7.5 cm (3 in) in diameter and 10 to 12 cm (4 to 5 in) in height, and were encased in individual muslin pockets, then clipped together with 'hog' rings to give a unit of a size suitable for the interior of a cushion, or an arm or back. They were also sometimes used as the top layer of springing for a double sprung seat; this type of springing is still used today, mainly in the higher quality spring interior mattresses.

The end of the Second World War saw many changing conditions in the upholstery trade. In the UK, the Utility scheme operated by a government department known as the Board of Trade had limited the supply of materials and the amount of labour which could be employed to make domestic furniture during the war years, thus also restricting the freedom of design. By the time restrictions were raised the cost of materials, manufacturing and labour had all risen considerably. There was also a shortage of skilled upholsterers able to continue the work. Manufacturers therefore favoured the introduction of methods which would enable a more economical use to be made of the available labour and reduce the degree of skill needed in the various jobs.

The modern approach to upholstery, particularly the greater use of mass production techniques, has led to a decline in the number of apprentices fully trained in all aspects of upholstery, but although the major part of the upholstery trade currently works under mass production conditions, there is, nevertheless, still demand for the

2 Upholstered settee with latex cushions: the seat is webbed with resilient rubber webbing, and the back may be upholstered with rubber webbing or serpentine springing

3 Modern style of chair upholstered with polyether foam formed into rolls of differing sizes; a central metal strut runs through each roll connected to a central metal spine; the covering is of expanded vinyl (courtesy of the London College of Furniture)

4 Foam shapes with a covering tailored in black vinyl to form a seating arrangement and day bed (courtesy Harold Hunt LCF)

highly skilled craftsman and for custom built work using the traditional materials and methods of construction.

A high rate of production in most cases is achieved by the use of preformed or sheet materials and some form of suspension unit which is easy and quick to apply. The use of these commodities results in a considerable saving in time when compared with the traditional method of teasing loose filling, and the time-consuming sewing and lashing of coil springs.

The changes over the years in methods of production also involved upholstery frame construction. For instance, the Victorian style of button back chair was frequently constructed in a combination of metal and timber, the back being made of steel rod and metal laths strongly fixed to a timber seat frame. This method, which was used at that time because it was easier for the blacksmith to produce the compound curves of the back in metal than for the curves to be shaped from timber by hand, was time-consuming for the upholsterer's frame-maker and fell from favour when woodworking machinery became available for the easier shaping of timber.

The use of metal for upholstery frames came to the fore again after the last war when difficulties in obtaining suitable supplies of timber were still acute but when steel, of which there was a surplus, and steel working machinery left over from war production were readily available. However, one of the major difficulties in the upholstering of metal frames has always been the attachment of the interior

11

materials and covering. Although in some instances this can be overcome by the fixing of timber fillets in appropriate positions the problems involved often meant a longer production time than was necessary when working with an all-timber frame. So the use of the metal frame lost popularity once again. Contemporary designers frequently favour a tubular construction of chrome, or angle iron, utilising a modern method of suspension for seat and back cushions, thus avoiding the problem of fixing any interior fillings to the metal framework.

5 Pressed steel easy chair frame produced in the post-war period (late 1940s) due to shortage of timber

6 Timber inserts fixed to a metal frame for tacking or stapling on materials

7 Steel frame incorporating a rubber diaphragm platform seat suspension (courtesy Pirelli Ltd)

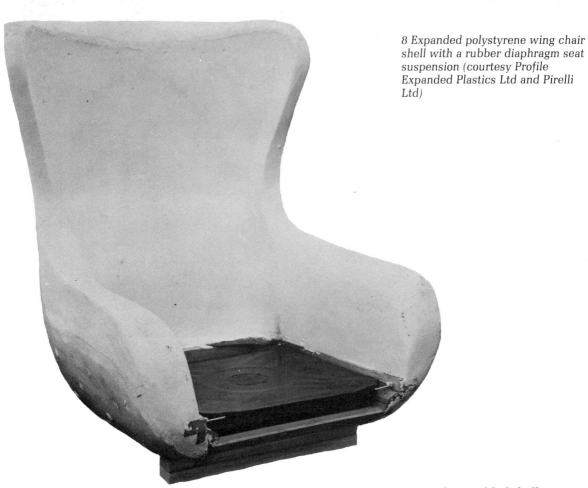

8 Expanded polystyrene wing chair shell with a rubber diaphragm seat suspension (courtesy Profile Expanded Plastics Ltd and Pirelli Ltd)

A current mass production technique is the moulded shell interior. This is moulded from expanded polystyrene or rigid polyurethane. The earlier styles of chair made by this technique were rather bulky, utilising thick section mouldings for greater strength; present day production methods however enable them to be stronger and more elegant with slimmer lines. In most cases, of course, the moulded shell requires a suitable fixing for a metal stand or underframe, unless it is particularly designed to reach floor level.

Workroom Practice

Health and Safety

In Britain, the Health and Safety at Work Act of 1974, administered by the Health and Safety Executive, lays down rigid regulations regarding working conditions in any place where people are employed. In order to ensure that the regulations are carried out as far as is reasonably practicable, employers are required to designate a safety officer to be responsible for overseeing the health and safety of the workforce. While the main responsibility of ensuring the safety of the workers rests ultimately with the employer, the employed themselves also have a responsibility towards their own safety and that of others.

One regulation states that if a worker who has been trained in the safe usage of a particular item of equipment which has been provided with adequate safety guards fails to use the guards provided, or ignores safety instructions given to him, and an accident occurs through this, the accident will be deemed caused by negligence on the part of the worker. Further, workers have a responsibility to one another regarding safety: a worker must not indulge in practices which could cause injury to another. It is also an offence against the regulations and renders a person liable to prosecution if he interferes with or damages any guard, safety device or equipment provided for fire-fighting by an employer for the safety of the workforce.

Inspectors from the UK Factory Inspectorate have the authority to visit and inspect business and factory premises regarding their compliance with the Health and Safety Regulations. These inspectors have the power to apply a warning notice to an item of apparatus or machinery with a time limit for any modifications required to bring the item up to the standard of safe usage as determined by the Health and Safety regulations. In extreme cases an immediate prohibition notice can be applied by an inspector with legal penalties if this is not complied with. This could also apply to a health hazard in any particular area of a workplace where the standards of dust or fume extraction do not come up to the requirements of the Act. An employer is also liable for the health and safety of any person visiting his establishment throughout the time they are on his premises; the employer, as far as is reasonably practicable, must make every effort to safeguard them from injury in any way.

Suppliers of materials have a duty under the Act to bring to the notice of users of their materials any health, safety or fire hazards involved in the use of these materials.

The points from the Health and Safety Act outlined here are just a few of the numerous regulations contained in the handbook produced by the Health and Safety Commission. An individual working on his own, not having an overseer to remind him of the dangers inherent in his work, does have to be aware that even the

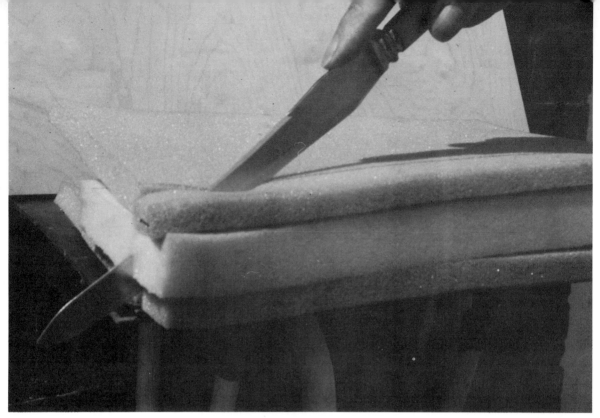

9 Cutting polyether foam with a
domestic carving knife

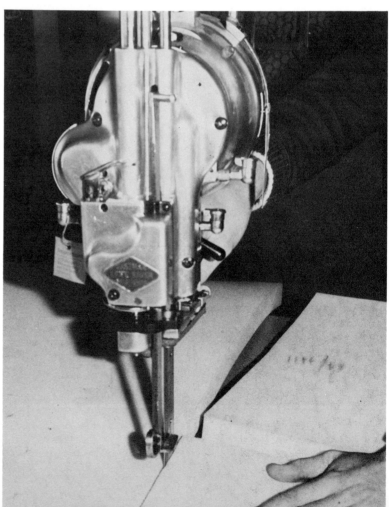

10 Cutting polyether foam with an
Eastman electric hand cutter

simplest operations sometimes have an element of risk if undertaken without due care and attention. This, of course, is true of some work in the upholstery field.

Professional standards

The craft of upholstery requires infinite patience and a certain amount of manual dexterity. Unlike wood, which is solid in form, most upholstery materials are flexible and often difficult to manage by someone with little previous experience. Very rarely is it possible for a novice to complete a difficult piece of upholstery to an acceptable professional standard.

Until recent years, practical benchwork has been considered a predominantly male occupation with females generally supplying subsidiary services such as sewing coverings, making and filling cushions, and slip stitching. In the United States men are employed as sewing machinists as well as women, particularly in the mass production field. In the United Kingdom it is usually only in the smaller units or shops with two or three workers that the upholsterer will undertake his own cutting and sewing machining.

There is a great temptation when fabricating the interiors of upholstered work to cut and form shapes and to undertake other interior work rather haphazardly and in a slapdash manner without due regard to professional 'tailoring'. This is often due to impatience on the part of the worker and results in irregular lines, uneven surfaces and poor outlines showing through the top covering, all of which give an unprofessional finish. Any uneven line in the covering will soil and wear more quickly than the surrounding fabric so it is essential to do the groundwork properly.

Wherever possible templates should be used. For example, before cutting out any foam or covering which needs to fit accurately, cut a paper or cardboard shape which can be tested for fit. Only when you are satisfied that the fit is exact should you go ahead and cut the foam or covering with confidence. A little extra time spent in this way will invariably pay dividends and save alterations later.

Whatever method is to be used for cutting foam, whether you use broad-bladed knife or an electric cutter, the final edges of the foam must be cut clean and square, not left with jagged edges.

In order to become adept in the use of the various materials and to get to know how they are used in the construction of upholstery it is wise to undertake simple projects initially and work up gradually to more difficult work. A series of upholstery projects, from the very simple to the more advanced, has therefore been included in this book as a guide to readers, who are advised not to be in too much of a hurry to undertake the more difficult (and this often means the more expensive) items: spoiling a piece of work through inexperience can be costly in terms of confidence as well as financial outlay.

Tools

The tools required by the individual craftsman to undertake modern upholstery work are few compared with those needed by other craftsmen. A number of major and minor mechanical appliances are available for many kinds of operation in the full scale production of modern upholstery, some operated manually, some electrically and others by compressed air, the latter now being used extensively in modern furniture making.

The professional upholstery manufacturer with a fairly large production unit will, of course, generally invest in any type of equipment which will speed production. The smaller producer, or perhaps the one-man business, undertaking a modest amount of modern upholstery will be able to cope with a minimum amount of equipment.

The stapling of upholstery materials on to timber frames, chipboard, hardboard, etc, has over the last decade virtually superseded the tacking method for modern work. Using staples is far more economical than using tacks; it is speedier in mass production and far more convenient. Staples, however, are not as easily removed as tacks, especially if applied with a compressed air gun into beech, the usual timber used for upholstery frame making. A small staple extractor specifically made for the removal of misplaced or damaged staples is therefore a valuable tool.

Diagram 1
Upholstery tools: (a) scissors, (b) buttoning needle, (c) magnetic hammer, (d) ripping chisel, (e) mallet, (f) circular needle, (g) trimming knife, (h) regulator, (i) flat staple extractor, (j) upholsterer's skewer, (k) staple extractor

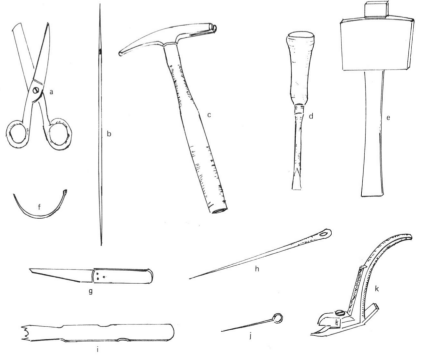

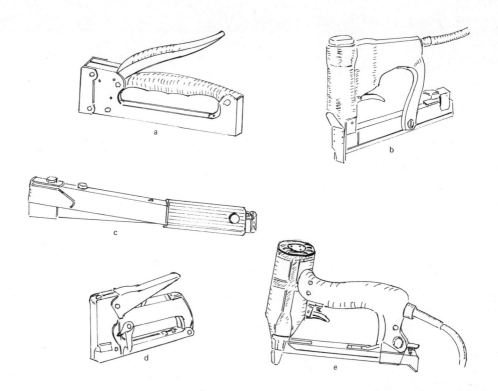

Diagram 2
Stapling tools: (a) McGill's hand stapler, (b) Senco pneumatic staple gun 'J' series, (c) Roberts stapling hammer, (d) Copydex hand stapler, (e) Lawson electric stapler

There are a variety of types of staple guns available for upholstery and other work. It must be stressed that only the heavy duty guns and staples are suitable for upholstery work; the common paper stapler will have insufficient power to punch the staples into hard timber and the staples will generally fold up before entering the timber or hardboard. It is wise to take care in buying a good stapling tool; some of the lighter spring-loaded types supposedly intended for this sort of work quickly lose their firing power as the spring weakens and this generally leaves the staple protruding to some extent, which means that the material is not firmly attached.

While it is usual for upholsterers working on modern furniture to staple foam and fabric to the frame, there are some who still prefer using a hammer and tacks. Either method may be used successfully.

The number of tools needed to undertake modern upholstery depends upon the type of work, and whether it includes the application of foam and a covering complete stripping and modernising, foam and cover cutting, internal construction of the basic upholstery, or simply minor frame repairs, alterations and modifications.

The following list of tools are those which will be required for most types of major work.

Metre or yard stick
Tape measure
Tailor's chalk (white and
  coloured)

Felt-tipped marking pen
Scissors, 20 or 23 cm (8 or
  9 in)

Trimming knife (shoe-maker's, leather or Stanley trimming knife)
Broad bladed knife (for cutting foam)
Staple gun
Staple extractor
Upholsterer's hammer (magnetic or traditional type)
Ripping chisel
Mallet
Upholstery buttoning needle, 20 or 23 cm (8 or 9 in)
Fine circular needle, 8 or 9 cm (3 or 3½ in)
Upholsterer's regulator, 20 to 25 cm (8 to 10 in)

Upholsterer's skewers (20 or 30), 10 cm (4 in)
Abrasion disc with electric drill
Spatula (for adhesive application)
Brush (for adhesive application)

The following tools are also required for frame repairs or alterations
Cabinet hammer
Tenon saw
Hand or electric drill with suitable bits
Wood rasp
Pincers
Try square

11 Pneumatic studnailer—a modern method of applying decorative nails (courtesy Senco Pneumatics (UK) Ltd)

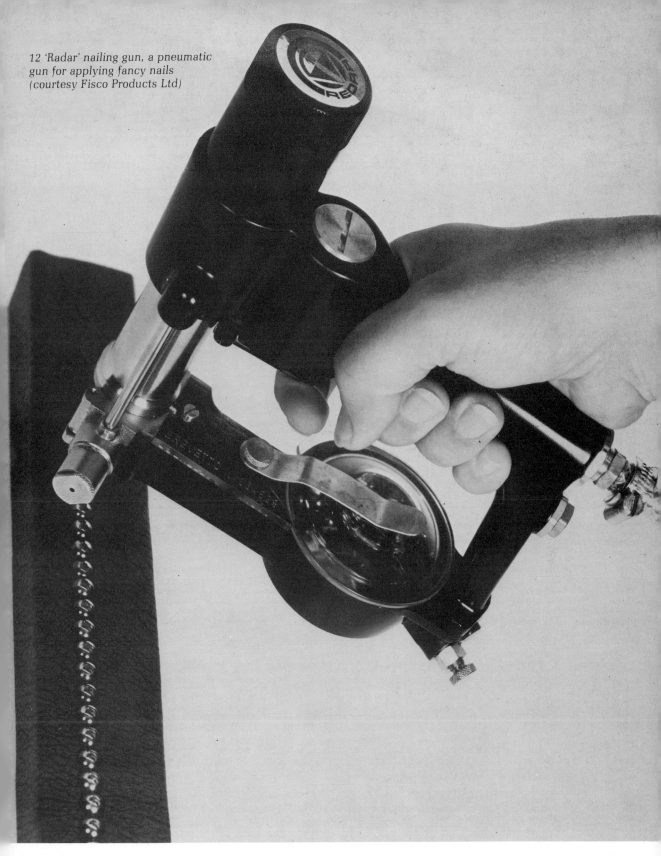

12 'Radar' nailing gun, a pneumatic gun for applying fancy nails (courtesy Fisco Products Ltd)

Materials

A student of any craft is a better student if he is aware of the range of materials that is available to him and knows how the various materials are best used, their advantages and disadvantages.

The secret of success in modern upholstery production is in the use of preformed units in fillings or suspensions. There are a number of traditional fillings which have been adapted for use in modern upholstery, these being manufactured into sheet or pad form so that they may be applied easily and quickly.

One of the greatest advantages in the use of preformed fillings for mass production is that a large number of units, such as easy chairs and settees, are reproducible in identical shapes and sizes because of the use of standard thickness sheets or shapes of fillings. This is not generally possible with the traditional loose fillings where individual upholsterers must use their discretion as to the amounts and densities of hair or fibre required. It is possible for two upholsterers working in the traditional way to produce finished chairs from identical frames looking quite different in shape and size.

There are some basic commodities which are frequently used in various ways in both modern and traditional upholstery: jute and linen webbing, jute hessian, calico, linter felt, tacks and gimp pins. Staples and foams are used almost exclusively in modern work.

Jute and linen webbing

Used when 'hand' springing a seat or back, jute and linen webbing can also be used in conjunction with foam (diagram 41). Linen webbing, normally 5 cm (2 in) in width, is made from a mixture of flax and cotton fibres (herringbone striped). It is of a better quality than jute webbing and consequently more expensive but is well worth the additional expense as it has a far longer life.

Jute webbing, brown in colour rather like hessian, has a looser weave than its linen counterpart, tends to deteriorate much quicker and will fray or wear if allowed to abrade or rub against an edge of the frame. It is not advisable to use this webbing on load-bearing areas if a long lasting construction is contemplated. It is sometimes used in widths greater than 5 cm (2 in); 7.5 cm (3 in) widths are frequently used.

Jute hessian

Generally known as canvas (burlap in the United States), this is obtainable in a number of grades or qualities, the poorest grade being a very loose and open weave with little strength for load-bearing. This quality is frequently used on the underside of upholstered items to cover the raw edges of covering tacked on the bottom of the frame, the hessian being folded under and tacked or stapled on.

The better qualities of hessian are used for lining the inside and

22

outside of arms and backs of chairs, to reinforce the covering and prevent it from being pushed in and becoming slack (diagram 75). (Plywood may be used for the lining of inside arms instead of hessian, diagrams 69 and 70).

Calico

A lightweight, unbleached white cotton fabric obtainable in various qualities, this is used as an undercovering. While it is not absolutely essential to apply an undercovering, it is good practice to use calico over the foam of seats, backs and arms because it allows freer movement of the top covering material than would the foam itself, which tends to drag or grip at the top cover. A further advantage of using a calico undercover is that with some types of velvet there is a tendency for the pile to be dragged from the cotton background weave and an undercover will prevent this from happening. Also latex foam will deteriorate fairly quickly if bright sunlight is allowed to filter through a loosely woven covering fabric onto its surface; a closely woven undercovering, such as calico, will prevent the latex surface from crumbling prematurely.

Linterfelt

A thick lap of cotton fibres, frequently used in traditional work and as a form of padding in mass production upholstery, linterfelt is laid over timber surfaces as insulation instead of foam. It is supplied by weight in rolls of approximately 12 m (13 yd) which come in varying thicknesses, an average thickness being 3.6 cm (1½ in). Linterfelt should not be used over foam because it has a tendency to break up if used on a surface which is too flexible.

Tacks

Where a staple gun is not available, the alternative is to use hammer and tacks. A certain amount of judgment is required in the use of tacks and the selection of the most suitable size for any particular stage or operation. The range of tacks available and generally used for upholstery is as follows.

16 mm (⅝ in) improved
16 mm (⅝ in) fine
12 mm (½ in) improved
12 mm (½ in) fine
10 mm (⅜ in) improved
10 mm (⅜ in) fine
6 mm (¼ in) fine
12 mm (½ in) gimp pins
10 mm (⅜ in) gimp pins

Diagram 3
Improved and fine tacks: the thicker shank and broader head of the improved tack is for coarser materials, and the more slender fine tack for stronger, tight weaves

The difference between improved and fine tacks is that the improved tack has a larger head and a thicker shank than its fine similar-length counterpart. In deciding whether to use the improved or the fine tack, consider the type of the material. If the fabric has a tight or close

23

weave and a strong yarn, choose a fine tack. If the fabric has a loose weave and a weak yarn, the improved tack would be more suitable.

A further consideration is the section or thickness of the frame timber. If the timber is lightweight or small in section, and looks as though it might split easily, it will require fine tacks; on thicker timber improved tacks can safely be used.

Experience teaches the upholsterer which size of tack to use for each job: for example, fine tacks are easier to drive into hard beech than improved tacks. A general guide is to use the smallest tack which you consider will hold the material successfully. The very smallest tacks, i.e. 6 mm (¼ in), are normally used only for thin plywood or hardboard, as these will not protrude on the reverse side.

Gimp pins

Gimp pins, 12 mm (½ in) and 10 mm (⅜ in), are available black-japanned and in a number of colours. They are used for fixing 'gimp', and wherever it is desirable to fix materials with a pin the same colour as the fabric, which will blend in with the weave and not show up against it.

Staples

Where stapling is used to fix materials a plentiful supply of staples should be to hand, and it is important that these should be of the type specifically intended for the particular gun being used. Staples come in a wide range of sizes and vary in length (leg length) and width (crown size). The two leg lengths most commonly used in upholstery work are 10 mm (⅜ in) and 6 mm (¼ in), the longer leg length being used for the thicker materials or where the materials have a lot of strain or tension applied to them. In some instances where thin plywood or hardboard is being employed, staples with a shorter leg length should be used, i.e. 3 mm (⅛ in). The usual width of staple (crown size) is 12 mm (½ in).

Staples will have greater holding properties if they are inserted at a slight angle from the straight (approximately 15°) so that the points do not enter the material along a single line of weave; the slight angle will allow the points to grip a number of threads.

Staples should also be used rather closer together than tacks, depending on the operation being carried out and type of material being used. Generally, when a single thickness material is being fixed, staples should be inserted rather more closely than when a folded material is being attached. To give a completely satisfactory fixing of fabric or similar material a spacing of approximately 12 to 18 mm (½ to ¾ in) should be used. Where little tension or strain is to be applied, wider spacing may be permissible, but over-spacing can be a false economy and cause materials to break away from their fixing points at an early stage.

Diagram 4
The range of staples supplied for a Senco 'J' series pneumatic staple gun runs from a prong depth of 2 mm to 12 mm (³/₃₂ to ½ in)

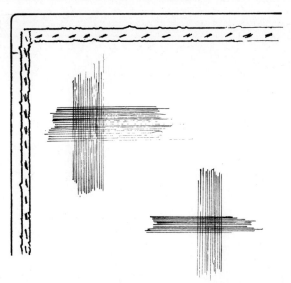

Diagram 5
Staples should be applied at a slight angle to encompass more yarn for added strength

Foams

There are two basic foams used for modern upholstery—latex foam and polyurethane foam—and these are two completely different products. There is a third, important type, known as reconstituted foam, which provides firm cushioning in particular instances.

Latex foam. Latex foam is manufactured by whisking up natural latex, the milky sap from the rubber tree, to a froth to entrap air within the liquid, pouring the liquid into a mould and baking in an oven—a process developed by Dunlop in the late 1920s. Latex foam is generally available in three forms. *Pincore sheet* comes in sheets 2.5 cm (1 in) to 10 cm (4 in) thick or thicker if required. It is moulded with fine pencil-shaped holes which give added softness and ventilation. *Cavity foam* is produced in sheet form 36 mm (1½ in), 50 mm (2 in) and 62 mm (2½ in) thick with one smooth surface and cavities on the reverse side. Cavity foam is now mostly used for seating for cars and commercial vehicles. *Solid sheet,* in thicknesses from 12 mm (½ in) to 25 mm (1 in) is smooth both sides. Latex foam is also produced in moulded form in a variety of shapes as required.

Diagram 6
Latex cavity foam: two sheets forming a cushion with a square of solid latex between to give a domed appearance; solid sheet is also glued around the sides to give smooth walling

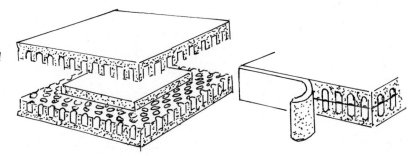

Currently the most popular of the three types of latex is pincore sheet, because it may be readily cut into shapes with only minor indentations around the side borders. In this it has a great advantage over cavity foam, the larger cavities of which cause uneven sides

25

13 An arm being upholstered using pincore latex foam: note how the jig is used for convenience of handling

Diagram 7
Latex cavity foam used in car seat upholstery

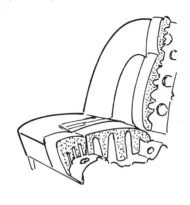

after cutting, and therefore need walling with 12 mm (½ in) solid sheet if smooth sides are to be obtained. To make a cushion from cavity foam, face the cavities together so that the two upper and lower surfaces are smooth, then join the edges with 12 mm (½ in) sheet foam to the full width of the border.

Polyurethane foam. Polyurethane foam is a product initially developed in Germany and the United States during the 1940s; it was later produced in the United Kingdom on a large scale. Polyurethane foam is made from by-products of the petro-chemical industry. The constituents are mixed together, and instantly form a gas which reacts on the liquid causing bubbling, so that the liquid expands and quickly gells into a large 'bun' or block with a cellular structure of controlled density and hardness. It is then cut into sheets of various thickness and fabricated into shapes to suit production needs. Different densities and types of foam may be used to vary the degree of firmness needed at different points of pressure.

The adhesive used to glue the cut parts of foam together is normally applied by a spray gun specifically designed to apply a particular adhesive. There are a number of types of spray guns available for this purpose.

The most widely used polyurethane foams in upholstery are polyether and polyester. The former is now solely used for cushioning in upholstery and bedding, while the latter is used to back laminated

26

fabrics, often for upholstery coverings and fabrics with other end uses.

The secret of success when using both latex and polyurethane foams is the selection of the correct density for a particular use; in large scale upholstery production it is vital to get the seating comfort right. A considerable range of densities of foam is offered by the manufacturers, and they will offer advice on the appropriate density and hardness to use in any given situation.

A further factor to bear in mind when choosing foam for a piece of work is the thickness of cushioning needed. This will mainly depend on the type of suspension being utilised for both seat and back.

Reconstituted foam. Reconstituted foam, or chip foam as it is frequently called, is firmer and denser than normal polyether foam, having different deflection characteristics, and is used in different ways.

Reconstituted foam is manufactured from off-cuts of polyether foam chipped up into small crumbs and introduced into the normal foam mixture at the foaming stage so that the chips are bonded together with the gelling of the mixture. Produced in continuous block form, it is cut into convenient sheets as required by the foam processors. Foam manufacturers produce two, three or four different densities, from a medium hard to a very hard foam. This foam may be cut in a similar way to other foams, but thicknesses of less than 18 mm (¾ in) are difficult to cut without the sheets breaking up.

Reconstituted foam is very useful. It may be used as a firm padding on seats which have a solid base where normal polyether would 'bottom', for example on typist's chair seats which are in use for long periods and thus require a firm support. It may also be used as a firm base with a layer of softer polyether over the upper surface. A further use for reconstituted foam is for walling softer foam where the edges of a soft foam would collapse with the tension of the covering. The firmest grade of reconstituted foam is frequently used for the filling of gymnastic pads and mats.

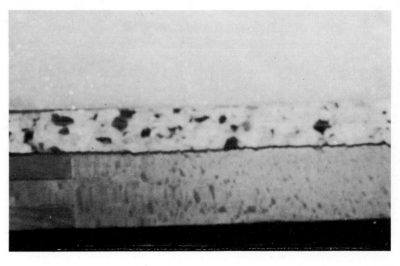

14 Reconstituted foam is used between the soft surface foam and the chair frame to prevent 'bottoming' of the soft foam

15 Reconstituted foam used to reinforce the edge of soft foam on a seat

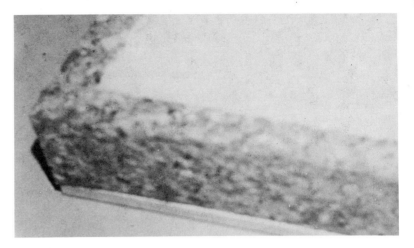

16 Reconstituted foam used as a sandwich with two soft outer surfaces

(facing page)
17 Reconstituted foam can be used to give firm lumbar support at the bottom of a chair back

18 Reconstituted foam is used here as firm edging for a hammock-type chair

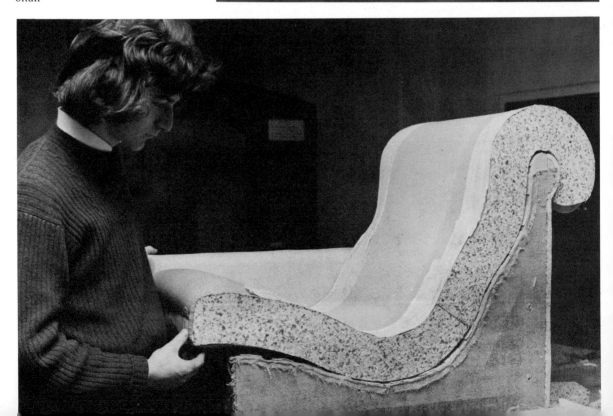

Dunlopreme polyurethane foams

Dunlopreme colour and number	Density KG/M³	Density LB/FT³	% compression set 75% deflection BS 3379	Grade BS 3379	Grade BS 4443	Main application areas
D1 Light blue	14/16	0.88/1.00	10	8A	2 & 3	Low density, soft grade. For use under light covers in backs and headrests where very little load bearing is required.
D2 White	14/16	0.88/1.00	10	8B	3 & 4	Low density foam. For quilting and applications where very little load bearing is required.
D3 Light green	17/18.5	1.05/1.15	10	8C	3 & 4	Low density, medium/soft grade for backs, arm panels and mattress toppings and quilting under soft cover.
D4 White	19.5/21.5	1.22/1.34	15	8A	2	Super-soft, slow recovery foam, ideal for pillows and for very soft toppings. Can also be used as core material for wrapped back cushions.
D7 Pale yellow	21/23	1.31/1.44	10	8D 8E	5	A low density, medium hardness foam. For arm paddings, wings and firm backs.
D8 Light grey	23.5/25.5	1.47/1.60	10			A medium density, firm hardness foam developed for use in the motor industry. Not recommended for furniture cushioning. Suitable for arm pads.
D9 Turquoise	25/27	1.56/1.69	8	8D 8E	5	A medium density, medium hardness foam for general cushioning.
D10 White	27/29.5	1.69/1.85	8	8C	4	A medium density, soft foam excellent for mattresses and back units. Can be used as soft cushioning or as a core material on middle-price upholstery.
D11 (Dulon) Lilac	30.5/32.5	1.90/2.03	8	8A	2 & 3	A high density, very soft foam for plump soft cushioning or for use as a wrap over firmer cores. Although very soft it can be used for full depth cushioning on suitably designed frames and platforms.
D12 Gold	27/30.5	1.69/1.90	8	8E 8F	8	A medium density, medium hardness foam for general upholstery cushioning, loose cushions, cores for firm fibre-wrapped cushions and arm pads.

Dunlopreme polyurethane foams

Dunlopreme colour and number	Density KG/M^3	Density LB/FT^3	% compression set 75% deflection BS 3379	Grade BS 3379	Grade BS 4443	Main application areas
D13 Peach	27/30.5	1.69/1.90	8	8F 8G	6	A medium density firm foam for use in the motor industry and as firm cushioning in quality upholstery. Can be used where firm padding is required or as a platform over springs. Can also be used as a firm edging around softer grades.
D14 Dark green	30.5/32.5	1.90/2.03	6	8C	3 & 4	A high density foam good for high quality back units. Especially useful for convertible units, where softness is required as a back and a mattress. Ideal for domestic mattresses. Suitable for soft cushions or as a soft core for wrapping when used on suitable flexible platform or sprung base.
D15 Pink	34.5/37	2.16/2.31	6	8D 8E	5	A high density grade for quality cushioning, or core for fibre wrapping. Suitable for contract seating and use on solid bases in sufficient depth.
D17 Steel blue	48/51	2.97/3.15	6	8E 8F	5	Premier quality foam. Medium/firm hardness. For heavy load bearing applications: theatres, hotels, restaurants and areas of hard use. Excellent high quality cushioning with good fatigue resistance.
D36 Pale pink	17/19	1.05/1.19	10	8A	2	A low density, soft grade for use as headrests, soft backs or as a wrap for back cushions.
D40 Light green	23.5/25.5	1.47/1.60	10	8C 8D	4	Soft, medium/low density foam for arm padding, wings and backs.

Reconstituted 'Repol' (Chipfoams)
A range of four grades

DR62 Blue	60/68	3.75/4.25	10			Soft. For use in dining or typist chairs where thin but firm padding is required. Walling of soft polyether.

Dunlopreme polyurethane foams

Dunlopreme colour and number	Density KG/M³	Density LB/FT³	% compression set 75% deflection BS 3379	Grade BS 3379	Grade BS 4443	Main application areas.
DR63 Yellow	80/88	5.00/5.50	10			Medium. Used for packaging and firm padding as above. Walling of soft polyether.
DR64 Orange	96/104	6.00/6.50	10			Hard. For very firm padding and agility or yoga mats.
DR65 Grey	96/104	10.50/11.50	10			Extra hard. Used mainly for gymnastic pads, judo mats, etc.

Methods of Springing and Suspension

Webbing and hessian (canvas), known as burlap in the United States, have been used to make up seat bases from the early days. Prior to 1828 upholstery was without springing, and the webbing, hessian or filling was applied to the top surface of the seat members and referred to as the 'top' stuffing of a seat.

Coil springs

Coil springs were introduced into uphostery seating to give it more depth and resilience. 'Double cone' springs, made up of coiled springs narrowing at the centre, were used. These springs are also sometimes called 'hour glass' or 'waisted' springs.

The spring unit.   The 'spring assembly', a framework with a number of coil springs already assembled and made to a size to fit into the seat of an upholstery frame, was patented in 1904 and successfully launched into the upholstery trade. This proved to be the first of the many preformed 'aids' to modern upholstery which were developed in later years. The modern spring unit is still widely used in contemporary mass production where a depth of springing is required at a nominal cost without employing the laborious hand-springing method.

Diagram 8
Unit springing: a seat springing unit fixed to the frame with steel laths using single cone springs for deep springing

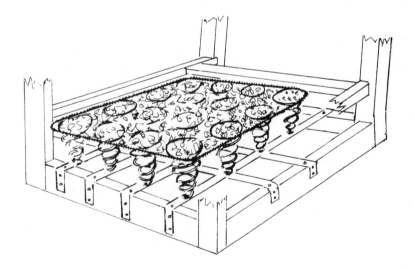

Tension springing

Elongated closed coil springs are used to provide tension springing. These fit between the holes of steel plates or eyeletted tape screwed to the side members of the seat or back. The springs should be applied or hooked on to the side plates under tension of approximately

33

19 Tension springs on the back of a chair showing the heavier gauge of the lower two springs; the covering hessian should be slack

8%. For a seat or back with a width between plates of 45 cm (18 in) a spring 3.6 cm (1½ in) shorter should be used. Springs used for seat springing should be of heavier gauge than those used for backs; 14 SWG (standard wire gauge) for seats, 18 SWG for backs.

Side plates of average length will usually have sufficient holes to accommodate nine springs. In some instances plates will have two holes close together on the front end to allow the greater support of having two springs close together on the very edge of the front of the seat; this is to prevent sagging.

Tension springs may be of plain metal finish which necessitates some form of apron as a covering to avoid an unsightly appearance when the cushion is removed or may have a tight brown plastic sleeve over each length. They may also have a covering (generally brown) formed from cotton yarn which is woven around the spring as it is being formed and this covering is woven in such a manner that it will stretch as the spring expands.

Replacing old springing. A disadvantage of this type of springing is that it can easily be over-extended with misuse, for instance, standing on the seat springs with the weight concentrated on one or two strands of spring only will cause them to become unserviceable so that they need replacement. Should this happen, it will usually be best simply to strip all the springs off the side plates, unscrew and

34

remove the plates, then replace the springs with resilient rubber webbing, as this will be easier to obtain than a new set of tension springs.

If you do decide to fit new springs and cover them with hessian, put some pleating in the hessian to allow for the deflection of the springs. If this is not done the hessian will have a hammock effect and cause the springs to be ineffective.

20 Overstretched and unserviceable springs in a chair seat

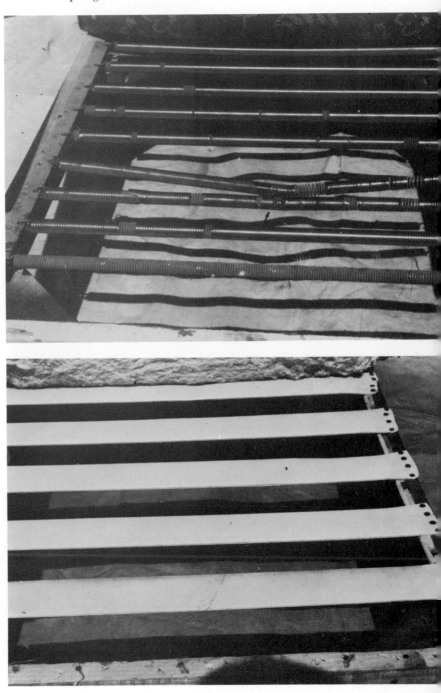

21 Rubber webbing can be used to replace tension springs

Rubber cable. A similar effect to that of the metal tension springs may be obtained by the use of thick rubber cable in a continuous length threaded from side to side through holes in the side seat members. Recessed slots on the outer surfaces will accommodate the cord to avoid any projections through the covering along the sides of the seat.

Serpentine springing

Serpentine springing is sometimes referred to as sinuous springing, or by the patented trade names of the manufacturers of the springing, 'No-Sag' or 'Zig-Zag'. Used extensively in modern upholstery for the springing of seats and backs, it is formed from tough steel wire into a series of 'U' bends in a continuous length of springing. It can be supplied to upholsterers in coil lengths of approximately 30 to 45 m (100 to 150 ft) or cut to specified sizes. A special wire cutter and spring length gauge is available, which simplifies and speeds up the mass cutting of lengths of springing, thus avoiding individual measuring of every strand.

22 Measuring and cutting arrangement for serpentine springing

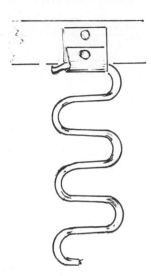

Diagram 9
Serpentine springing, showing the fixing clip nailed to the frame

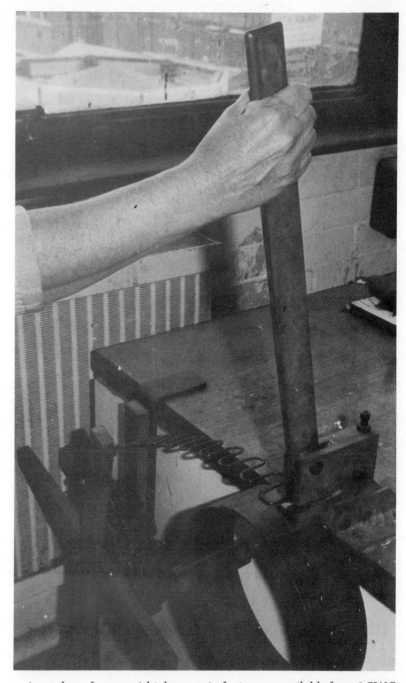

23 Serpentine spring wire cutter in action

A number of gauges (thicknesses) of wire are available from 8 SWG to 13 SWG, including the intermediate ½ gauges. In general the longer spans between seat rails will require heavier gauge springing with shorter spans—loose seat size—using the lighter gauge wire. A 30 cm length using 11 SWG and at the other end of the scale, say, 68 cm (2ft 3 in) needing 8 SWG springing. The lighter gauges are recommended for backs. Where units are formed from the springing, lighter gauges of 12 and even 13 SWG may be utilised.

24 Serpentine spring back unit for a chair

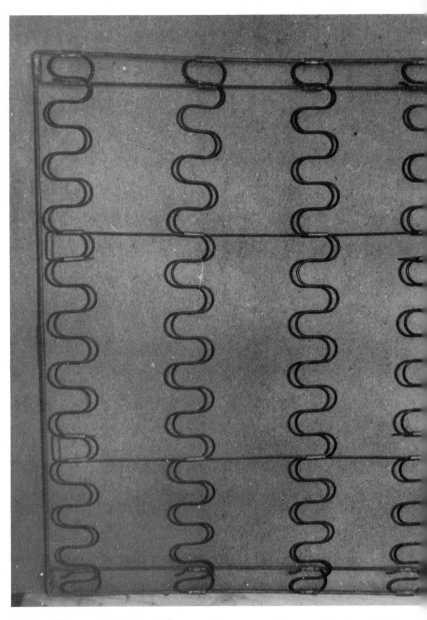

Fixing the springing. When using serpentine springing it is important to remember that an arc must be retained in the springing after it has been attached to the upholstery frame and that the frame must be soundly constructed to withstand the tension of the springing: seat rails to which the springs are attached should be at least 25 cm (1 in) thick to avoid any bowing of the timber inwards.

Due to its method of construction the springing will naturally form an arc which can be varied depending on the total length of the spring between the fixing points on the frame. The greater the arc left in the spring after fixing, the greater the amount of deflection or springiness the seat or back will have. Suitable arcs will vary from approximately 3 cm (1¼ in) to 6 cm (2½ in).

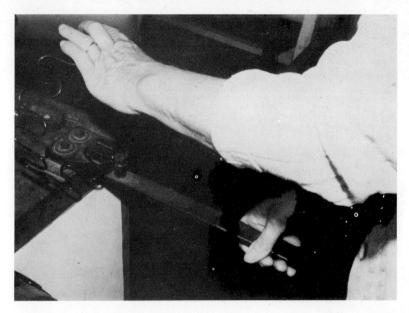

The ends of the spring must be bent after cutting in the centre of a
'U' bend to prevent the end of the spring from slipping out of the
fixing clip; this also prevents the projecting wire from fouling the
edge of the seat rail. A special bending tool is available which
simplifies this operation.

In the construction of a bar seat, a long sofa or a divan, to carry a
mattress, it is necessary to take special precautions to prevent the
long front and back seat rails to which the springing is fixed from
bowing inwards, particularly on the upper edge.

Diagram 10
*The typical arc formed by
serpentine springing fixed to a frame*

Diagram 11
*Reinforcement of the frame to
prevent bowing of the front and
back rails when using serpentine
springing: (a) by fitting a cross
member, (b) by fitting braces.*

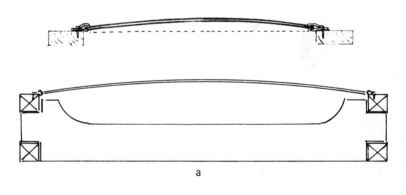

a

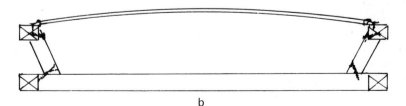

b

Resilient rubber webbing

Designers of modern upholstery often call upon the upholsterer to provide seating with a cushion but with little depth of seat to carry the cushion. Luckily there are methods of forming a seat with reasonable resilience with a minimum depth of support.

Laminated resilient rubber webbing is probably one of the most versatile and easily applied materials used in modern upholstery. The technique of using the webbing and fixing it in position can quickly be mastered by both the professional craftsman who has never used it before and the amateur. Because of this it has become very popular in the DIY market and is readily obtainable in the standard quality and the popular widths of 5 cm (2 in) and 3.6 cm (1½ in) and, in most cases, in two colours, natural rubber colour and black. Other widths and colours are available from upholstery warehouses. It is sold by the metre (yard) or roll.

'Laminated' rubber webbing is made up of a number of layers or laminations, five in the case of the standard and super grades of webbing. The laminations consist of three layers of rubber with two layers of rayon cords sandwiched between them. The advantage of this form of construction is that with the tensioning of the webbing, as the rayon cords are on the bias, or set diagonally within the webbing, they prevent over-stretching of the webbing, giving a gradual restriction on the elongation as the tension is increased. This prevents excessive sagging or deflection if a particularly heavy person sits upon the seat. In this respect laminated rubber webbing reacts somewhat like an upholstery double cone coil spring, which has increasing resistance with heavier loading.

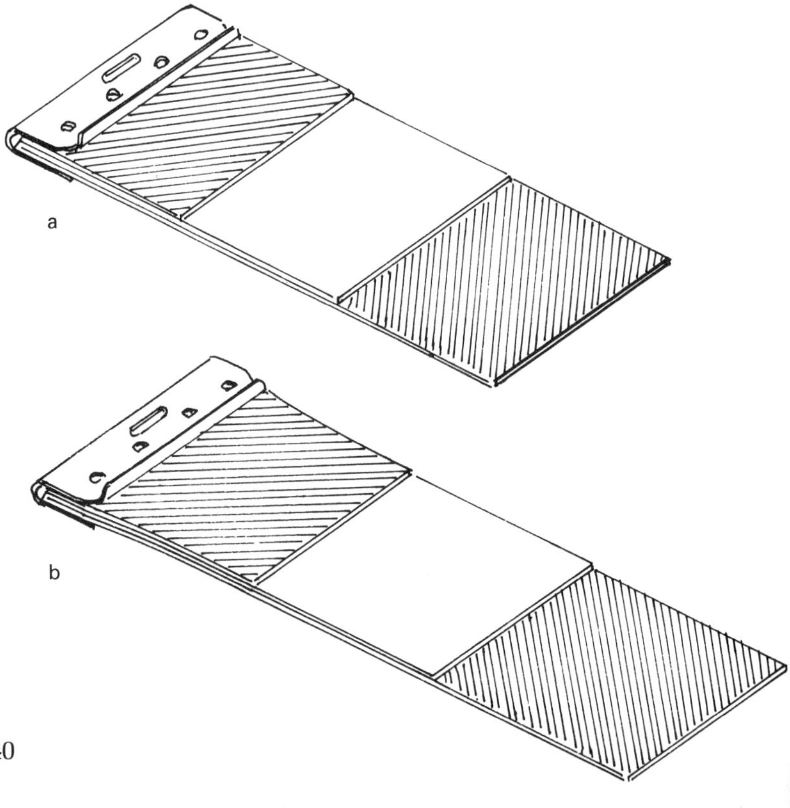

Diagram 12
(a) The inner rayon threads that prevent over-extension of laminated resilient rubber webbing
(b) Slight narrowing of webbing due to applied tension. Note changed angle of Rayon threads

Fixing the webbing. Laminated rubber webbing may be attached to seats and backs of timber upholstery frames with normal 12 mm (½ in) or 16 mm (⅝ in) tacks of the fine type, or staples with 12 mm (½ in) leg. It may also be attached by means of pressed steel clips which are clamped onto the ends of the webbing after it has been cut to the desired length. This method of fixing necessitates having a groove cut in the side members of the seat into which the steel plates fit. To accommodate the clip it is necessary to cut a mortice or continuous slot 16 mm (⅝ in) deep and 4 mm ($^5/_{32}$ in) wide in the top of the side seat rails. The slot must be angled inwards by about 15° (75° to the underside of the webbing); the clip may then be inserted easily by hand. The clip must not be hammered into position in the slot as this will damage the webbing.

Diagram 13
Applying the steel fixing clip to resilient rubber webbing

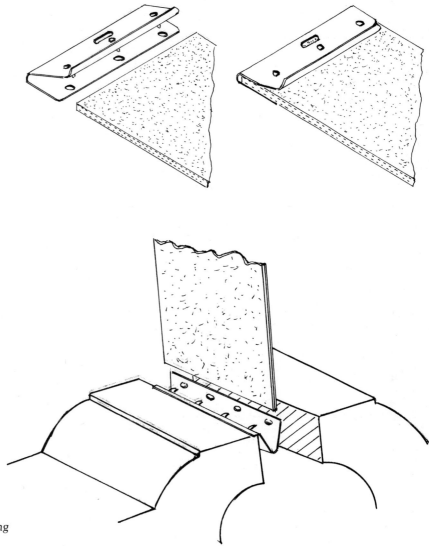

Diagram 14
Closing the clip onto the webbing with the aid of a metal vice

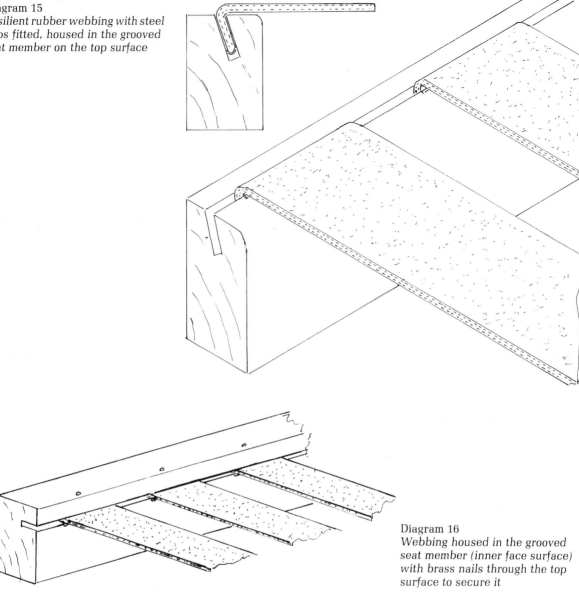

Diagram 15
Resilient rubber webbing with steel clips fitted, housed in the grooved seat member on the top surface

Diagram 16
Webbing housed in the grooved seat member (inner face surface) with brass nails through the top surface to secure it

As an alternative to being fixed to the top of the seat frame the slot may be machined on the inner faces of the side members using the same type of pressed steel clip but with the clips held in position by a panel pin hammered carefully into the timber so that the pin enters through the centre slot in the clip the slot is elongated to allow for easy location of the pin).

A useful recent addition to the range of fixing clips is a slightly modified type known as the 'mortice' clip. Diagram 17 shows how webbing fixes into mortices to accommodate a single web; a special tool is needed to insert the clip so that it locks itself into the mortice slot. This clip is fitted onto the end of the webbing in exactly the same way as the standard type.

42

Diagram 17
The mortice steel clip, a late
introduction to webbing fitting

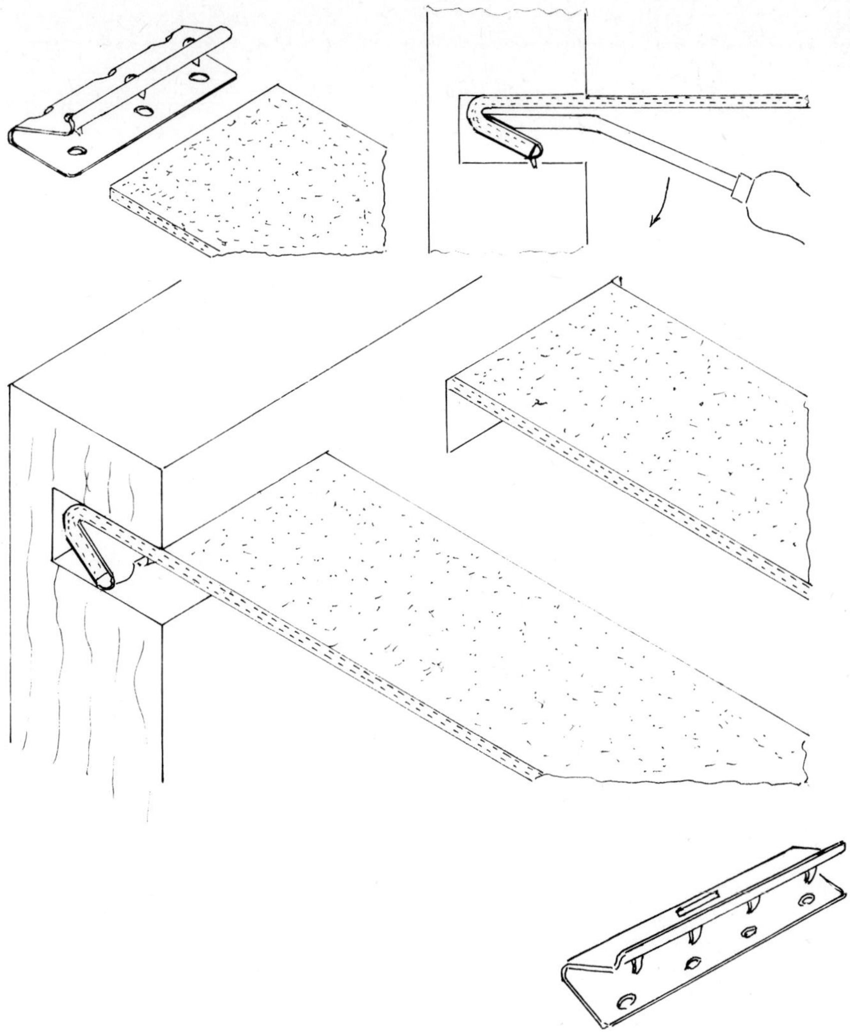

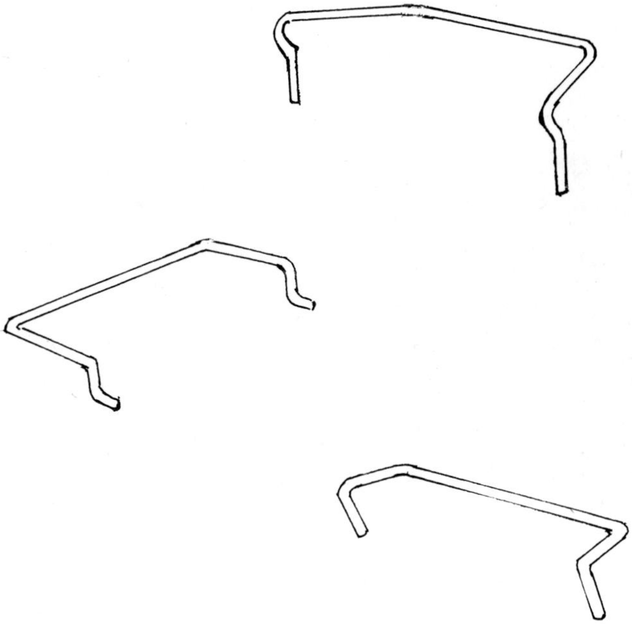

Diagram 18
Different types of wire hooks for
fixing rubber webbing to metal
upholstery frames

For steel tubular or angle iron fixings there are a number of different types of wire hooks which fit into holes drilled into the metal frame. The webbing is fixed to the hooks by wrapping round and passing a wire staple through the folded webbing with flat metal plates either side for reinforcement. A number of methods of using the wire hooks on metal frames are shown here.

Diagram 19
Attaching rubber webbing to wire hooks

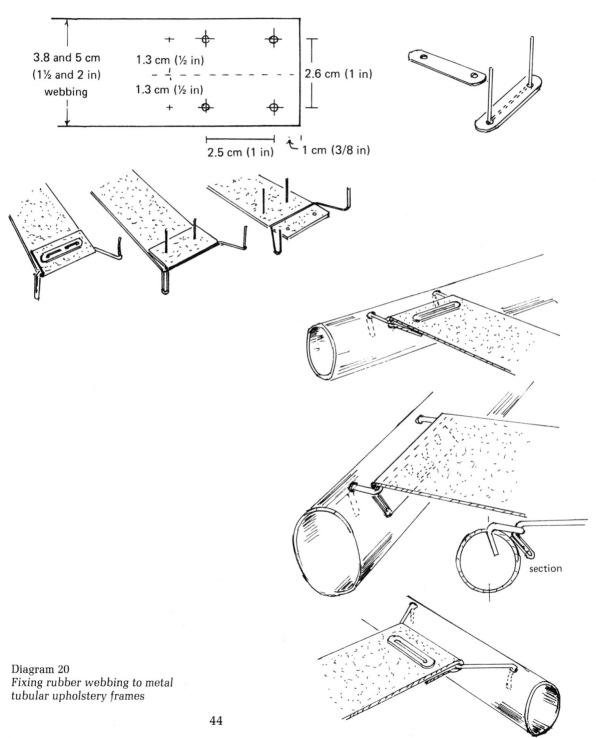

3.8 and 5 cm
(1½ and 2 in)
webbing

1.3 cm (½ in)

1.3 cm (½ in)

2.6 cm (1 in)

2.5 cm (1 in)   1 cm (3/8 in)

section

Diagram 20
Fixing rubber webbing to metal tubular upholstery frames

44

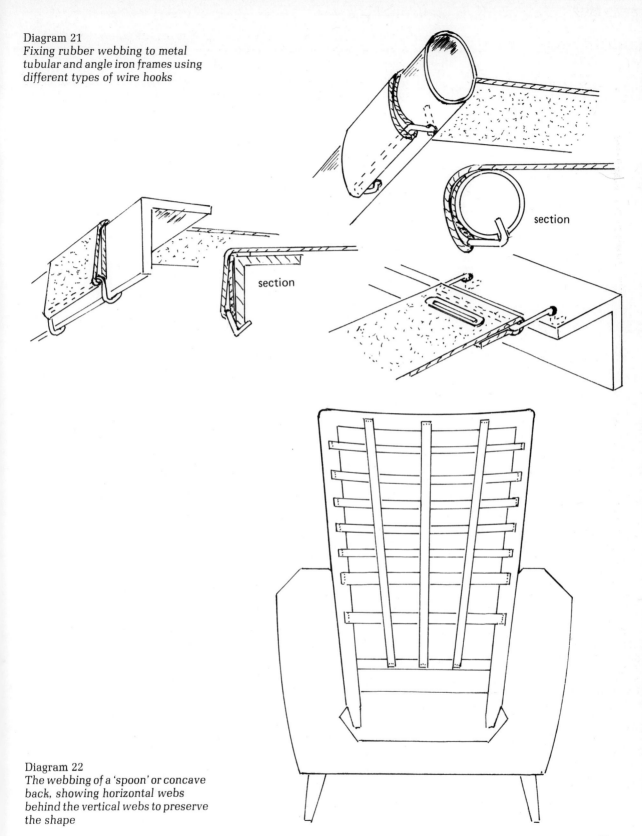

Diagram 21
*Fixing rubber webbing to metal
tubular and angle iron frames using
different types of wire hooks*

section

section

Diagram 22
*The webbing of a 'spoon' or concave
back, showing horizontal webs
behind the vertical webs to preserve
the shape*

Tensioning the webbing. Tensioning the webbing is important. To function correctly the webbing must be under tension; the firmness of the seat or back is directly related to the amount of tension given to the webbing—the tighter the webbing is stretched, the firmer the seat or back will be. The following table gives a guide to tensioning webbing for different widths of seats and backs, for hard, medium or soft results. The figures given are for the 5 cm (2 in) standard quality webbing and the lengths of webbing include 12 mm (½ in) each end for fixing by stapling or tacking, or, if the steel clips are to be used, include the amount which clamps into the clip.

It is necessary, of course, to cut each strand exactly the same length to ensure an equal tension on each strand once it has been fixed into position, unless the seat or back is tapered, or narrows towards the back of the seat, or to the bottom or top of the back. If this is the case, the amount of tapering should be allowed for in the cutting and fixing of the webbing.

Tensioning table

Seat span	Hard	Medium	Soft
457 mm (18 in)	419 mm (16½ in)	432 mm (17 in)	444 mm (17½ in)
483 mm (19 in)	444 mm (17½ in)	457 mm (18 in)	470 mm (18½ in)
508 mm (20 in)	447 mm (18½ in)	483 mm (19 in)	495 mm (19½ in)
533 mm (21 in)	495 mm (19½ in)	508 mm (20 in)	520 mm (20½ in)
559 mm (22 in)	508 mm (20 in)	520 mm (20½ in)	546 mm (21½ in)
584 mm (23 in)	533 mm (21 in)	546 mm (21½ in)	559 mm (22 in)
610 mm (24 in)	559 mm (22 in)	570 mm (22½ in)	584 mm (23 in)

Try fixing and marking each strand on the frame so that they may be tensioned equally as an alternative method to that of marking the lengths along the roll before fixing. This involves tacking the first end, marking the webbing at the inside line of the frame, making a further mark on the webbing indicating the amount of tension, then stretching the webbing and fixing with the inner mark at the edge of the frame.

Generally, laminated rubber webbing can be used without interlacing strands, providing the length is not excessive, i.e. over 60 cm (24 in), and providing the strands are reasonably close together, approximately the width of a strand apart. Interlacing tends to restrict the springiness of the webbing: where the strands cross they will grip each other if they are used in both directions. Interlacing may be advisable, however, for certain jobs, for instance where a very firm seat is required or on a curved or 'spoon' (concave) back.

Covering the webbing. Wherever possible the webbing should be covered as this will undoubtedly prolong its life. When, as often happens, the webbing is left uncovered apart from a cushion on the upper surface, it is easy to see how much more quickly the rubber left exposed to the light deteriorates than that which is covered.

26 Marking rubber webbing to assess the amount of tension on each strand

27 Rubber webbing tensioned to the correct amount

Rubber diaphragms

This extension of the resilient webbing concept comprises specially designed reinforced rubber platforms of a suitable size to fit between the corner stiles of a seat which have special hooks screwed into them; 'D' rings vulcanised into the corners of the rubber platform fit over the corner hooks. The platform should be under tension so that it

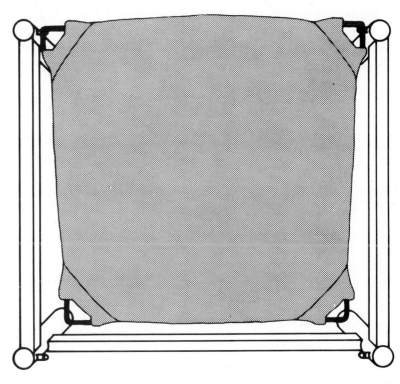

Diagram 23
Rubber diaphragm partly tensioned and fixed to a single seat unit (courtesy Pirelli Ltd)

47

Diagram 24
Rubber diaphragm tensioning tool
(courtesy Pirelli Ltd)

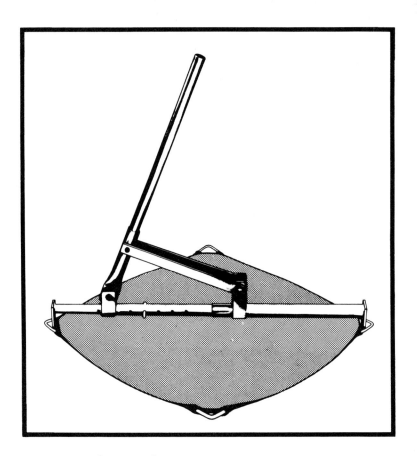

is taut across the seat; there is a special tool to help you achieve a suitable tension. It is very difficult to put the 'D' rings onto the corner hooks by hand, but the tool is able to stretch the platform diagonally.

The diaphragms are manufactured in easy chair seat sizes only. If you are seating a settee therefore it is necessary to arrange it in such a manner that each seating position utilises its own diaphragm; consequently positions for the hooks to hold the 'D' rings must be provided.

Replacing a diaphragm. Rubber diaphragms tend to deteriorate over a period of time and will sometimes split and need replacing. Unfortunately the platforms are not readily obtainable other than through upholstery supplies warehousemen or through the original suppliers of the upholstery.

An alternative for this type of suspension could well be resilient rubber webbing if fixing rails are in suitable positions or new rails for fixing can be put into the seating areas to give satisfactory support to the cushions.

Other types of suspension
Some of the other types of suspension used for seating in modern upholstery include 'Fabweb' suspension for timber frames and 'Sisiara' suspension for tubular frames (manufactured by Pirelli Ltd.).

48

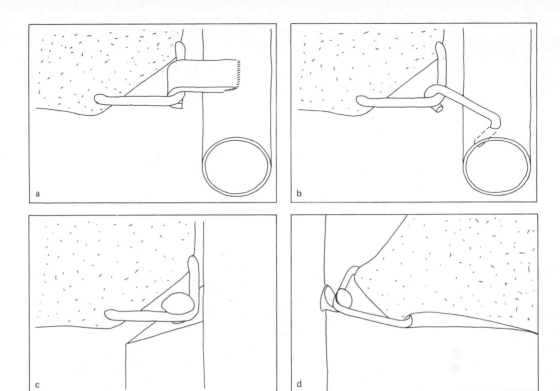

Diagram 25
Diaphragm fitting: (a) with a hook
welded in position on a tubular
frame, (b) with a hook inserted in a
hole drilled in a tubular frame, (c)
with a stud fitted into a timber frame,
(d) with a hooked stud on the back
strut of a timber frame

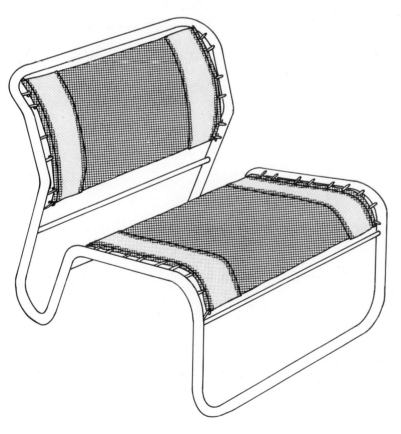

Diagram 27
Sisiara, a patented modern seat and
back suspension for tubular frames
(courtesy Pirelli Ltd)

Diagram 26
Fabweb, a patented modern seat
and back suspension for a timber
frame (courtesy Pirelli Ltd)

Cushions

Preformed fillings

An important development in modern upholstery has been the introduction of materials which can be supplied in a preformed state. The time-honoured traditional method of upholstering was always with loose fillings, such as horsehair, fibre, kapok, feathers and down. These can be difficult to manage when they are being applied to a seat, back or arm, even for the professional upholsterer, and call for a considerable degree of skill and craftsmanship, not only in handling but also in gauging how much to use. The appearance of the finished article will depend to a large extent on the amount of loose filling used.

The introduction of preformed materials, some of which are made from the original loose fillings in a compressed state, has been invaluable in the faster production of upholstered chairs and settees and has been a great help in attaining standardisation of the various parts of a chair and its cushion or any other type of work. This is possible because the preformed commodities are supplied in standard thicknesses which only need cutting to size and shape, fixing upon the base and covering to achieve the exact result desired.

Foam. The most common and frequently used layered filling is foam as it is both easily obtainable and easiest to use.

Linterfelt. Used in both traditional and modern upholstery, linterfelt, a thick padding of cotton fibres, is often laid over timber surfaces as insulation instead of foam.

Rubberised hair This is produced in sheets 183 × 90 cm (6 × 3 ft), 2.5 cm (1 in) to 10 cm (4 in) thick, a convenient size to cut into shapes for upholstery purposes, and is formed from a hair mixture (horse and hog hair) sprayed with liquid latex (rubber) so that the hair strands are bonded together in a homogeneous mass. The thinner sheets may be cut to size and shape with scissors but thicker sheets need a long broad-bladed knife or electric knife.

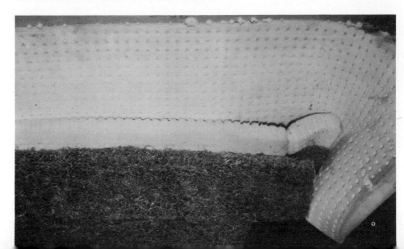

28 Rubberised hair being used with a pincore latex overlay

Rubberised hair may be used in a number of ways to give a lively resilience over a solid base or some form of springing. It does, however, lose some of its liveliness in a reasonably short period under constant or extreme use, particularly in a warm or humid situation.

Polyester fibrefill One of the most popular fillings of this sort is Dacron (Du Pont (UK) Ltd). Manufactured from white polyester crimped fibre, it is often more expensive than other forms of filling but it has exceptional 'loft' or bulkiness and resilience, is odour-free and is not weakened by cleaning fluids. It may be used in a number of ways in cushion construction and also as insulation or padding in upholstery work.

The fibre is obtainable in various forms for a number of uses and in different weights or thicknesses:

(a) as sewn batting with a fibre weight of 600 g per sq metre (18 oz per sq yd);
(b) as plain batting with a fibre weight of 600 g per sq metre (18 oz per sq yd);
(c) as skin bonded batting with a fibre weight of 600 g per sq metre (18 oz per sq yd) and 300 g per sq metre (9 oz per sq yd).

The sewn batting has a woven cheesecloth on one or both sides with chain stitching in lines lengthways; both the stitching and the cheesecloth may be removed or included as desired when the batting is being used as a filling for cushioning or as padding for upholstery.

Plain batting is interleaved with paper to facilitate handling and to separate the layers of fibre; the paper should be removed before use.

Skin-bonded batting is sprayed on both surfaces with a very light film of resin. This tends to bond the outer fibres, forming a more manageable layer for certain operations.

Cushion construction

Seat and back cushions for upholstered chairs and settees were traditionally made with feather and down fillings in an inner case made from cambric or, alternatively, were made as 'squab' cushions with a filling of horse-hair in a case of hessian or scrim with twine stitching around the side borders. Both these methods of construction require a certain amount of skill and expertise, and are time-consuming. In modern upholstery production, however, cushion making has to keep pace with chair and settee production, and as most suites made today may carry from five to ten cushions, speedy methods of cushion making are necessary.

Cushions for contemporary upholstery are usually made from either latex or polyether foam; both these foams may be bought in moulded form with domed surfaces (to simulate a fully filled down cushion) in a number of stock sizes to fit average size seats and backs. Alternatively, sheet latex or polyether may be used; cushions may then be cut from a single thickness of the appropriate size, or formed from thinner sheets glued together or laminated with different densities, to attain the desired hardness or softness.

One of the early faults in the making of foam interiors for cushions during the beginning of the 1950s was the use of unsuitable densities and thicknesses of foam, resulting in an unacceptably high percentage of compression set, that is, loss of depth or thickness of the cushion within a comparatively short time, particularly on its leading front edge. Today, however, the foam manufacturers have a better understanding of the needs of the upholstery industry. The foams produced now can be relied upon to give good wear and to retain depth or thickness over many years provided thought has been given to the type and density which will be most suitable for the particular piece of furniture.

A wide range of densities is now available, and in the UK foams are subject to testing by the BSI (British Standards Institute). The results of two of the tests are included in the chart on pp. 30-32, one concerning the density per cu kg (cu ft), and the other the percentage of compression set; also included are the BSI grades for the various densities of foam.

If you buy polyether or latex foam casually from a source other than a normal upholstery warehouse the density or BSI grading of the foam may not be known and in this case you will have to be very careful: a bad purchase will be regretted in a very short period of time.

It is rare that one can purchase foam, other than pieces cut specially to order, to the actual measurements required, so it will usually need cutting to size after purchase. Before you attempt to cut the foam at all it is advisable to cut a template (a pattern of the correct size and shape) from paper or card to the precise outline of the finished cushion. Check the fit by laying the template on the seat to ensure that it fits snugly between the arms and in line with the front edge of the seat.

For a settee which needs two, three or four cushions, it is necessary to divide accurately the distance between the arms into equal parts depending upon the number of cushions needed, and either cut that number of templates or mark the seat by inserting lines of pins where the edge of the template is repeated across the width of the seat.

T-shaped cushions (cushions with projections on the front corners) are more difficult to shape and cut, and it is usually more economical to attach the 'ear' pieces with adhesive after cutting the main seat piece rather than to cut the complete cushion from a larger piece of foam which entails considerable waste.

Having produced the template one can work out the most economical way of positioning the cushion shape on the sheet of foam if more than one cushion is to be cut from it, then mark around the edge of the template with a felt-tip pen to give guide lines for cutting.

Cutting the foam filling   A foam interior for a cushion, whether latex or polyether, should be cut fractionally oversize to ensure that the fabric outer case will have a slight tension to prevent wrinkles appearing. The average easy chair seat cushion interior should be cut 6 to 10 mm (¼ to ⅜ in) oversize in both directions to give satisfactory tension to the outer covering. Care should, however, be taken not to cut oversize by too large an amount as this will cause bowing of the interior inside the covering.

The extent of oversize cutting should be added after marking around the template. It is a good idea always to cut the foam just on the outside of the marking lines so that the lines remain on the edge of the cushion foam after cutting; this will provide proof that the foam has been cut to the correct size and not undercut.

Where a professional electric cutting knife is not available an electric carving knife makes an excellent cutter for foam. A long, sharp, broad-bladed bread or kitchen knife will also cut foam satisfactorily, provided care is taken to hold the knife perfectly upright and square with the cutting line, just over the edge of the table. When cutting with a broad-bladed knife it is better to use firm strokes, drawing the knife upwards each time, rather than to use a sawing action which tends to give a jagged edge.

Remember that any unevenness will show through the outer covering and spoil the finish: Care taken in cutting foam will pay dividends as far as achieving a professional finish is concerned. When cutting latex foam, the knife will cut easier if lubricated with plain cold water—a wet rag drawn down the blade every three or four strokes will prevent the latex from gripping the knife as it is drawn through the foam.

29 Cutting foam cushion with a domestic knife

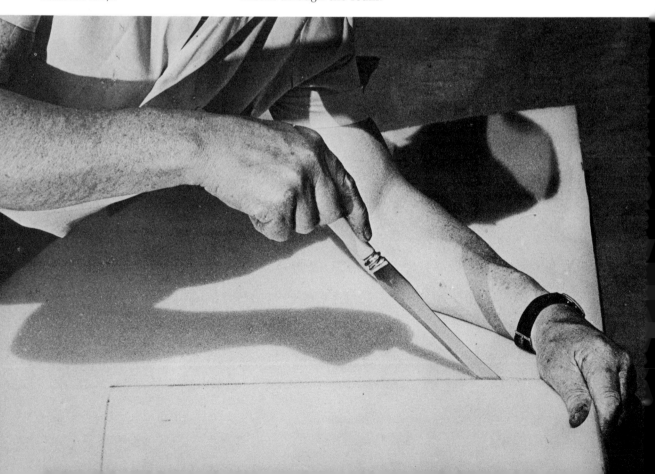

Making an undercover When making a foam cushion it is not advisable to cover the foam surface with cotton wadding or linterfelt. Due to the large amount of deflection and distortion to which the foam surface may be subjected during use, the wadding or felt would become torn and misplaced, resulting in a lumpy or uneven surface.

A latex interior, however, should have an inner case of calico or a similar, closely-woven, lightweight fabric to prevent strong light filtering through the outer covering and causing deterioration of the latex foam surface. There is no problem of this sort with polyether foam as this is not affected in the same way by strong light.

Applying a flange To ensure that the seam or piped edge remains neatly in place on a foam cushion, sew a flange of calico or a similar fabric onto the seam turning or edge of the piping across the front of the cushion. Alternatively sew it all round the top seaming or piping, and then glue this flange to the top edge of the foam interior.

If only the front edge of the cushion is to be treated in this way the opening for inserting the interior need only be across the lower back seam of the cushion case, but if the whole top seam is to be fixed to the interior filling the opening needs to be approximately three-quarters of the length of both sides in addition to the back to enable the covering to be turned while the interior foam is folded; care should be taken not to tear or split the covering during this operation.

Making a foam and fibrefill cushion

To give a softer and more traditional appearance to a modern cushion it is possible to combine foam with fibrefill, or to use fibrefill on its own; both simulate the feel and appearance of feather and down. Whilst the addition of polyester fibre adds to the expense, the result is well worthwhile, and obviates the hard straight lines so prominent with a plain foam cushion.

To make a cushion with a foam core and a fibrefill wrap, either latex or polyurethane foam may be used for the core. Illustration 30 shows a seat cushion constructed with a core of pincore latex foam with a wrap of plain Dacron fibrefill batting, covered with a case of

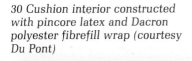

30 Cushion interior constructed with pincore latex and Dacron polyester fibrefill wrap (courtesy Du Pont)

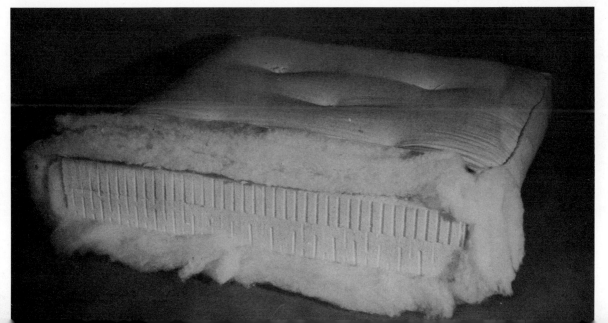

cotton scrim-cloth. Illustration 31 shows a section through a cushion constructed from a core of polyurethane foam with a wrap of skin bonded polyester Dacron 88 fibre. The plain fibrefill batting may be used over latex foam if desired.

The density of the core foam depends largely on the expected usage and the design of the seating. Generally, where shallow seats or hard front edges are to be cushioned the core should be of a reasonably firm foam; where there is a good depth of springing or supporting upholstery, a lighter density foam core may be used which will give a realistic simulated feather/down effect to the cushion. In any case, a foam should be selected which will prevent 'bottoming' of the cushion in use (the sitter completely flattening the filling to the base).

The size of the foam core should be carefully considered before you start to make up the cushion. Should the foam be cut too large it will buckle after it is inserted into the outer covering. On the other hand, an inner foam core cut too small will result in wrinkling of the outer cover through insufficient tension and you will have to resort to using a good deal of extra fibrefill to give the necessary bulk to the cushion. Ideally, the core should be of maximum size just short of buckling; 12 to 18 mm (½ to ¾ in) should be allowed for the fibre wrap, depending upon the density of the foam.

When only the top and bottom surfaces of a cushion are to be covered with fibrefill the foam core should be cut fractionally larger than the required length and breadth of the cushion to ensure that the covering is kept under tension to prevent wrinkling.

Where zipped removable outer covers are being used, the cushion interior of foam and fibrefill wrap should be encased in a woven or knitted scrim-cloth to prevent distortion or disturbance of the fibre while the outer covering is being replaced after cleaning. The scrim-cloth may be wrapped around the core and fibre without precise cutting and fitting, and the side and end edges sewn with strong thread using an upholsterer's slip-stitching circular needle.

Not so many demands are made of back cushioning as of seat

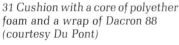

31 Cushion with a core of polyether foam and a wrap of Dacron 88 (courtesy Du Pont)

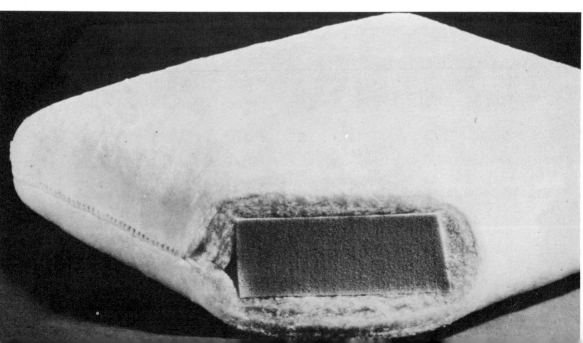

cushioning. The additional softness which is desirable for a back cushion can easily be attained by reducing the foam core thickness and density; generally, a back cushion thinner than the seat cushion is acceptable.

Making a fibrefill cushion

As an alternative to the traditional feather and down filled cushion or the foam core and fibrefill wrap interior, cushions may be filled completely with the polyester fibre Dacron. The ability of the crimped fibre to return to its original shape, thickness and appearance for a reasonably satisfactory period makes it ideal for modern upholstery cushions where a softness of the feather and down type is required.

Making a cushion in this way involves more work than the wrap method, as the case has to be machined. Illustration 32 shows a chair seat cushion made with 100% Dacron fibrefill; it shows the fibre contained in an inner case (made from calico or cambric) of three separate compartments with two divisions sewn from the upper to the lower panel. An equal amount of polyester fibrefill is rolled or folded and inserted into each compartment. The ends of the compartments may be left open (unlike a down cushion which must be completely sealed).

The width of the batting should be cut 15 to 25 per cent over the width of the finished cushion and the same is true of the length of the cushion. This should be filled so that it is 15 to 25 per cent longer before it is inserted into the outer case. For ease of handling the rolled fibrefill when inserting it into the inner case, it is convenient to wrap it in the scrim-cloth which is sewn to the batting in some cases.

Another good method of filling with 100 per cent Dacron involves using Dacron Type 88 at a weight of 460 g sq metre (14 oz sq yd). In this instance the layers of Dacron are stacked on top of each other until the desired density and thickness are achieved. The layers should be cut 30 to 75 mm (1¼ to 3 in) larger than the finished cushion.

32 Cushion made with 100% polyester fibrefill in three compartments (courtesy Du Pont)

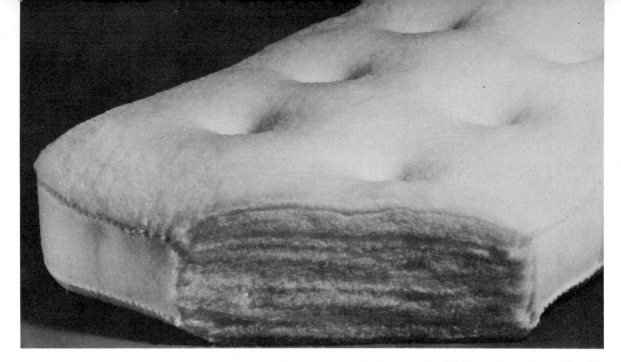

33 Cushion made from 100% Dacron 88 tufted (courtesy Du Pont)

For satisfactory wear the layers should be anchored together by inserting ties through all the layers or, alternatively, if the design of the cushion allows, by incorporating buttons as a feature of the finish so that the ties connecting the buttons will hold the fibre together. Sewing scrim-cloth around the border will also help to keep the layers in place.

Spring interior cushions A semi-traditional method of cushion construction is to use pocketed spring interior units with a wrap of polyester fibrefill. In some instances a pocketed cushion unit may be in a good condition but needing re-filling. Illustration 34 shows the unit with a wrap of polyester fibre which is much livelier than the cotton linterfelt which was normally used in the past.

34 Pocketed spring interior with a wrap of polyester fibrefill (courtesy Du Pont)

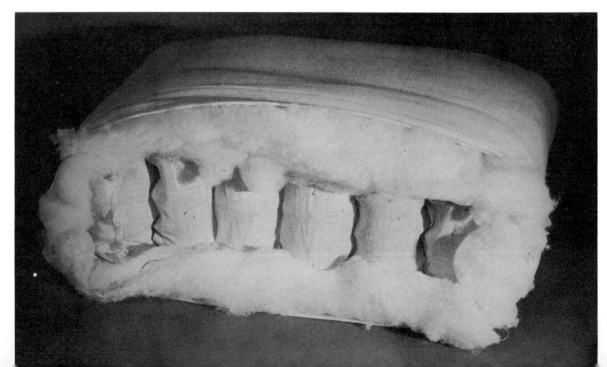

Adhesives

Types of glue

In the past the upholsterer relied very little upon adhesives, working as he did with materials such as hessian, scrim, coil springs, hair and fibre combined with timber frames. Adhesives were used in the making of the timber frame but the practical upholsterer himself needed adhesive only for the fixing of gimps, braids and fringes and even some of these were sewn in position. Animal glue was employed for both these jobs and the glue pot, gently simmering over a gas ring in the corner of the workshop, was a familiar sight — and indeed smell when the shopboy forgot to check the level of water in the lower pot, or someone turned the gas too high so that the water boiled dry and the glue burned.

Tube glue   Later, tube glue became popular; this was applied to the trimmings with the help of a wooden spatula (a small, flat spreader) which spread the glue thinly and evenly so that it did not work through the weave or overrun the edges of the gimp or braid. This type of adhesive is still manufactured and is still considered to be one of the best methods of fixing gimp or braid into rebates where covering has been tacked, giving a firm and permanent fixing.

Latex-based adhesives   Another adhesive which is suitable for this sort of work is a white latex-based adhesive (such as Copydex or Elmer's Glue-All). This is applied with a small brush which is supplied fixed to the lid if bought in a small jar. This type of adhesive needs rather more care in application and takes rather longer to set.

Choosing an adhesive   The development of modern upholstery materials, together with the general departure of the traditional timber frame called for a variety of different types of adhesives, since one adhesive could not be suitable for all jobs. For example, in the sticking together of flexible polyether foam there are some adhesives which will certainly stick the two pieces of foam together, but will leave a hard glue line along the join, and this hard line could well be felt through a thin outer fabric covering. While for a small job this may not be very important, where the work is on a large scale such a fault should be avoided by experimenting in the first instance; it should not be difficult to find an adhesive which will not leave a hard line in this way.

The modern adhesive industry has gone to great lengths and undertaken years of research to find a suitable adhesive for almost every conceivable gluing problem and there are very few materials which cannot be fastened together with adhesive. The major adhesive manufacturers are only too happy to solve any specific problems that arise in this field.

Modern upholstery techniques frequently involve the use of a moulded shell instead of a timber frame and it is important when using an adhesive on the shell to take care to select one that will be suitable for both the shell itself and the other material to be fixed to it, usually foam. Various materials are used in moulded shell production, e.g. glass-fibre reinforced plastic (GRP), rigid polyurethane and expanded polystyrene, and there are some adhesives, for example, which, if applied too liberally to expanded polystyrene, will cause its surface to disintegrate badly to some depth, causing cavities which

Dunlop Adhesives

	Aluminium foil	Cork	Fibreglass polyester	Hardboard	Leather	Metals & alloys	Latex foam	Natural fabrics	Paper & cardboard	Polythene	Polyurethane foam
Aluminium foil	S758	S758	S758	S758	S758	S758	S758	S758	S758	S957	S758
Cork		L107 A1020	S758	S758	S758	S758	L107	A1020	A1020	S809	L107 SN1249
Fibreglass polyester			S758 S691	S691	S691	S691	S758	S758 S888	S758	S957	S758
Hardboard				S758	S758	S758	SN1249 L107	A1020	A1020	S809	L107
Leather					S758	S758	L107	L107	L107	S957	S758
Metals & alloys						S758	S834	S758 S888	S758	S809	S758
Latex foam							S834 SN1249	A1020	A1020	S809	S834 SN1249
Natural fabrics								A1020	A1020	S809	A1020 L107
Paper & cardboard									A1020	S809	A1020
Polythene										S957	S809
Polyurethane foam											SN1249 S834
PVC flexible											
PVC leathercloth (cotton backed)											
PVC rigid											
Rubber											
Wood											

PVC flexible	PVC leathercloth (cotton backed)	PVC rigid	Rubber	Wood
S1115	S758	S691	S691	S758
S1115	S758	S758	S758	S889
S1115	S758	S691	S691	S691
S1115	S758	S758 S691	S758	S758
S1115 S1310	S758	S758	S758	S758
S1115 S691	S758	S758	S758	S758
S1115	S758	S758	S758	L107
S1115	S1115	S758	S758	S758
S1115	S1115	S758	S758	L107 S758
S957	S937	S957	S957	S957
S1115	S758	S758	S758	L107 S758
S1115	S1310 S1115	S1115	S691	S1115
	S758 S1115	S691	S691	S758
		S691 S758	S691	S758 S691
			S758	S691

will result in an uneven surface under the foam. The type of adhesive generally used for this purpose is Styrene Butadrene rubber based, a contact adhesive which is applied to both surfaces. There is not the same problem with rigid polyurethane moulded shells as both the flexible foam and the shell have the same origins.

The following chart has been compiled by Dunlop Chemical Products Division, and is given here as a guide to the major types of adhesive. Additional Dunlop adhesives for foam work are SN 1501, SN 1314, SN 1234 and SN 1249, the last being for roller coating application.

This table shows at a glance which adhesive to use for holding any material. Read down and across, and where columns meet is the adhesive type number.

Applying adhesives

There are a variety of ways of applying adhesives to materials in upholstery work, the method generally depending upon whether a 'one off' job or large scale production is being undertaken. Whichever is the case, attention must be paid to fire risks and to the dangers of solvent vapour. Adequate ventilation *must* be provided while work is in progress.

By hand Adhesive may be applied by brush, spatula, notched trowel or scraper. These instruments are inexpensive and suitable for the 'one off' job as no other equipment is required, but they do tend to use more adhesive than is strictly necessary; contact adhesive in particular should generally be used sparingly.

Roller coating This mass-production technique involves a grooved roller rotating in a reservoir of adhesive. The quantity of adhesive picked up by the roller and spread on the foam is controlled by a 'doctor' blade, or control roller, assisting in the spread of adhesive on the pick-up roller. The advantage of this method is the speed of application. The disadvantages arise where differing thicknesses of foam have to be coated and there can also be problems with evaporation of solvent and with cleaning.

Compressed air spraying This requires compressed air of approximately 6 kg per 52 cm (35 lb per sq in). In a modern upholstery production unit compressed air is normally piped to a number of working positions for compressed air staplers at a pressure of 13 kg per sq cm (80 lb per sq in). In these circumstances a spray gun position would need a reducer to drop the pressure of the air supply.

The principles of adhesive spraying are similar to those of paint or polish spraying. The adhesive is transferred from a container either by gravity feed or air pressure to the tip of the spray gun and atomised by the jet of air which is forced out in the form of a fine fan spray; this may be adjusted either horizontally or vertically.

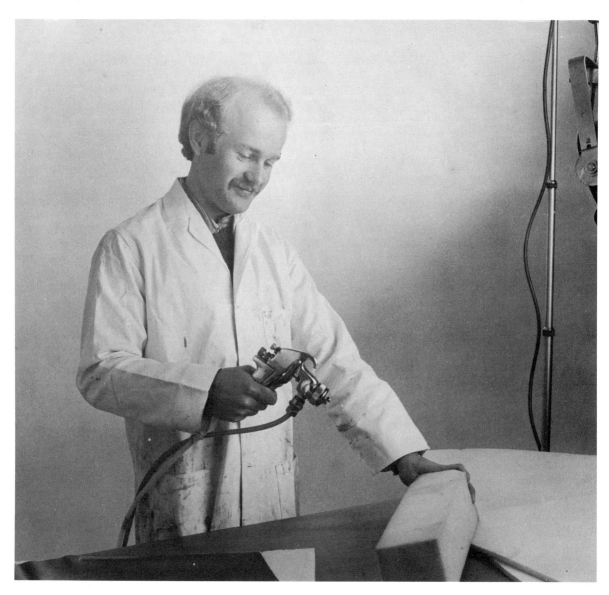

35 *Adhesive spray gun in use
(courtesy Dunlop)*

The advantages of this method are speed of application over large areas and economic utilisation of adhesive. A spray gun will apply a thin film of adhesive to both surfaces which may then be bonded instantly.

Airless spraying   This method of application tends to be cleaner and easier to control than the conventional spraying method.

Air is supplied to an air-operated motor which drives a pump immersed in the adhesive. The adhesive is then transferred at pressures of up to 454 kg per sq cm (2,500 lb per sq in) through a filter to the gun tip where it is atomised and sprayed in a fan spread, this being adjustable by means of fitting different tips.

The advantages of this method are even faster application than conventional spraying, absence of over-spray and air disturbance

62

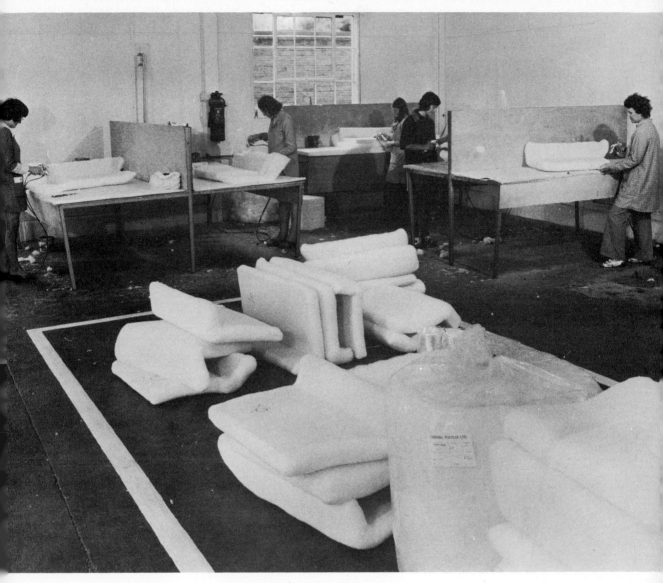

36 Part of an adhesive system in use at a commercial foam-building factory (courtesy Dunlop)

around the object being sprayed, and quick cleaning. The capital cost is relatively high so it is only economic for high production throughput; also, there are a limited number of adhesives which may be used.

Pressure extrusion spraying   This method involves the transfer of adhesive under pressure along a suitable hose to a pressure flow gun. The pressure transfer can be effected either by a pressure container or an air-operated pump. The method of transfer depends upon the viscosity of the adhesive.

The advantages of pressure extrusion spraying are that it is suitable for adhesives over a wide range of viscosities and that adhesive can be used direct from its special shipping container so that there is no loss of solvent.

63

Coverings

Types of covering

Selecting fabrics suitable for upholstery work needs careful thought and consideration. Fabric cost is generally the major outlay with upholstery work and choosing a fabric which does not have the right characteristics (handling or draping properties) for upholstery covering or, perhaps, selecting a material which does not have the necessary wearing or abrasion properties can lead to disaster.

Generally speaking, fabric made for casement (curtaining) use, for example, is not sufficiently hardwearing for upholstery covering and should not be used. Unfortunately, some departmental stores tend to mislead the public by selling 'furnishing fabrics' where they should distinguish between curtaining and upholstery.

In the past upholstery coverings have been woven from natural fibres with very little 'give' to them, the object being to produce something tough and hardwearing which would suit the traditional form of upholstery construction. The requirements or demands made of coverings for modern upholstery work have, however, changed somewhat in the post-war years with the introduction of new techniques and methods of production and the widespread use of foams. In the main, covering traditionally stuffed upholstery involved the tensioning of fabric over fairly straight firm lines or edges, the only really soft part of the chair or settee being the down or feather cushions.

In contrast, the covering of modern upholstery generally involves the casing of foams, some of which are ultra-soft. The efficacy of these foams will be lost if the covering is tensioned tightly or too heavy or too thick a woven fabric is used. Consequently, fabrics used today need to be of a lighter weight with softer and more pliable weaves.

Alongside changing upholstery techniques and the introduction of foams is the development of new fabrics from man-made fibres. A number of these not only ideally suit present-day upholstery styles and methods of production but also have improved handling, working, wearing and cleaning properties.

The most important consideration (apart from its visual effect) when selecting a fabric is, of course, its wearing properties, that is to say, its abrasion resistance. In the UK, fabrics specifically intended for upholstery use have the Martindale abrasion test figures (how the fabric has stood up to the rubbing test) printed on their specification. It is important to know the relative meaning of these figures to appreciate how the fabric will stand up to normal wear and tear.

A loosely woven, poor quality cotton fabric, such as a cotton repp or 100 per cent cotton uncut moquette, will most certainly be unsuitable as upholstery covering; if given the Martindale rub test it will have a poor result and, in fact, figures are seldom published for

the lower quality fabrics. A figure in excess of 40,000 rubs on the Martindale abrasion testing machine should be looked for in a fabric to give reasonable wear for upholstery use, particularly if piping of seams or facings is to be undertaken, as piping is generally applied to leading edges where wear is greater than in other areas.

Some good quality upholstery fabrics containing worsted yarns will prove to have extremely hardwearing properties and will stand up to 60,000 rubs or more. Coverings used for seating in public transport vehicles are specifically woven for the purpose, and will stand an excess of 100,000 rubs without showing signs of wear. Fabrics of that toughness are not, however, normally available for sale to the domestic upholsterer or amateur.

Traditional coverings for upholstery work have always been woven tough enough to give many years of hard wear, and to allow the upholsterer to tension the fabric over the fillings (which were stitched shapes filled with fibre or hair) without the covering tearing or splitting while it was being strained in a number of directions.

Modern upholstery, which invariably means using foam, does not usually involve this sort of tensioning and the fabric covering does not have therefore to withstand the same strain as in traditional work. Covering being applied over foam needs only very slight tensioning, so in many instances lighter and different types of fabrics may be used for modern work. The use of the traditional heavier type of material may indeed restrict the foam, and often prevent it from returning to its original depth.

Man-made fibres Man-made fibres feature extensively in the production of a large number of fabrics used as upholstery coverings suitable for modern production techniques using foams. It is interesting to see how the use of these fibres has developed in recent years. The following table shows the consumption of all fibres including natural fibres in the United Kingdom textile mills in 1960 and 1977.

Fibre Consumption in Textile Mills

1960		1977	
Wool	32%	Wool	17%
Cotton	37%	Cotton	14%
Cellulosic	24%	Cellulosic	18%
Nylon	4%	Nylon	21%
Polyester	2%	Polyester	16%
Acrylic	1%	Acrylic	13%
		Others	1%

Cellulosic fibres are those based on or originating from plant life, i.e. wood chips or cotton linters converted by chemical action and processed into filaments for the production of rayon.

There are a number of man-made fibre producers in the United Kingdom, Europe and the United States and all have their own trade marks and registered names. Fabrics woven with a particular man-made fibre will normally convey the trade mark name. The following list gives brand names for various types of man-made fibres.

Man-made Fibres

Fibre Type	Trade Mark		
Acrylic	Acrilan	Elastone	Lycra
	Courtelle		Spanzelle
	Orlon	Nylon	Bri-Nylon
	Dralon		Celon
	Teklon		Enkalon
Polyester	Dacron		Antron
	Diolen		Blue 'C' Nylon
	Lirelle		Perlon
	Terlenka	Polypropylene	Courlene
	Terylene		Cournova
	Trevira		Ulstron
Viscose rayon	Evlan	Acetate rayon	Dicel
	Sarille		Celafibre
	Viloft		

Preparing the covering

Fabric suitable for upholstery covering is normally 122 cm to 127 cm (48 to 50 in) wide. Some fabrics, quite often those made from man-made fibres are wider, up to 132 cm (52 in) wide. When estimating the quantity needed for a particular upholstered item, it is wise to assume that the narrower width will be supplied rather than to plan on the basis of wide width and find later that you do not have enough.

Layout   As covering is the most expensive item in most upholstery projects it is very important to plan the cover cutting layout completely before attempting to cut into the material: an error through thoughtless cutting can prove to be costly. If possible, draw a scaled-down cutting plan on squared paper so that maximum use may be made of the fabric without any waste.

For reasons of economy it is advantageous to work from the half width of the fabric. In many instances with easy chairs and parts of couches or settees it is possible to do this; for example each side of a cushion will, in most cases, come out of the half width (i.e. getting both panels out of the full width). Seats, inside backs, outside backs and occasionally inside and outside arms can also be cut from the half width.

Marking up   Tailor's chalk, rather than blackboard chalk, should be used to mark up the material. Blackboard chalk marks quickly disappear when the fabric is being moved around. Chalk lines should in most cases be made on the reverse side of the fabric. Wrong marking with tailor's chalk on the face side of fabric is difficult, and sometimes impossible, to remove. While most fabrics have the weaving yarn lines visible in both directions (warp and weft) it often is very difficult to cut along the weave accurately without guidelines.

Work from a cover cutting plan, marking the sizes to be cut on the covering with the tailor's chalk with strict regard to the weave: the selvedge of the fabric should be laid parallel to the edge of the cutting table. To keep the fabric still on the cutting surface pritchawls, skewers or clamps may be used; some fabrics do tend to slip about as you work.

Cutting out   The first important tool needed for this, is, of course, a good, fairly large and very sharp pair of scissors or shears. It is difficult to make clean, straight cuts into thick material with a small, blunt pair of scissors; you tend to get ragged edges which are difficult to work with. Good cutting is a vital element in the finished appearance of the work.

A metre stick (or yard stick) or some form of straight edge used in conjunction with a tape measure is an essential aid to straight cutting; lines should be drawn with the assistance of the straight edge and not drawn freehand.

The ideal cutting table is wide enough to take the whole width of the fabric and long enough for a good length to be laid out flat so that templates may be moved around on top of the covering to determine their best positioning. It is impossible to mark and cut covering accurately on a small dining table, particularly if the table is polished.

Machining

Machining upholstery coverings is not always necessary. Many small items, and indeed some larger ones, including easy chairs and settees, are designed in such a manner that the covering need only be laid on and fixed in position in one piece without any need for fitting, tailoring and machining. The majority of upholstery workshops employ specialist cover cutters (both male and female) and experienced machinists.

The secret of successful machining is in the preparation of the covering prior to machining. Assuming that the cutting has been completed correctly, with the aid of templates or chalk lines drawn on the fabric, the parts of the covering should be adequately pinned together and tried on the foam or prepared upholstery to ensure that a perfect fit will result. It is well worth taking a little time over this because this is the key to success; without this checking a lot of time may subsequently be wasted in making alterations.

Where there is any possibility of the fabric slipping or moving in either direction while it is being machined, a number of 'V' shaped notches should be cut into the edges of the fabric of both pieces to be machined and matched up during machining. This process is, of course, used in dressmaking and tailoring and anybody familiar with either of these skills should be able to undertake upholstery cover machining with confidence. A large number of upholstery machinists do, in fact, learn their skill in the tailoring trade, and move into the upholstery industry subsequently.

The lightweight domestic sewing machine is not usually able to cope with upholstery work, the fabric frequently being rather thick and bulky, particularly when there are up to four thicknesses of material to be machined together at one point, or when piping of the seams is being undertaken. Certainly, coping with leather would be beyond the ability of the normal domestic machine.

The industrial lockstitch machine which is probably used more than any other for upholstery work is the Singer 31 K15. Other machine manufacturers produce similar types and these will generally cope with most upholstery cover sewing requirements

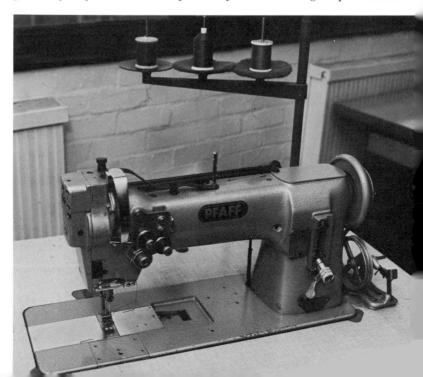

38 Flat-bed, twin-needle machine used for twin lines of decorative stitching on upholstery covers

39 *Post machine used for twin lines of decorative stitching on upholstery covers with compound curves*

including leather work. In the production of modern upholstery a variety of other special machines are used. For decorative, double-line stitching, the flat-bed twin-needle machine or the twin-needle 'post' machine is used. An overlocking machine is frequently used on detachable covers to prevent fraying of edges. The 'Tuftmaster' long-arm quilting machine is used to produce deep quilting on chair and settee back panels.

The best method of learning machining is to get plenty of practice in control of the machine before attempting to sew coverings at all. Draw straight and curving lines, making various shapes on stout drawing paper, then without any thread in the needle, machine over the lines: the performations made by the needle will show how successful in machine control you have been. Go slowly at first, speeding up only when you can follow the lines without deviation.

69

40 Singer three-thread overlocking machine, used for overlocking edges of upholstery covers to prevent fraying, particularly on detachable covers

41 The Apex Tuftmaster, a long-arm quilting machine for deep quilting of upholstery covers

The more familiar and confident you become with the controls, the more capable you will be of overcoming difficulties and problems in the work.

The machine should, of course, be kept well oiled but not over-oiled; any surplus oil should be taken up by machining a waste piece of absorbent cloth, this preferably being left under the pressure foot overnight.

When you are working with a thick upholstery fabric, the pressure foot may need adjusting (raising) to prevent undue wear. Also use a heavier gauge needle for thicker fabrics.

Use the correct thread for the job. A good deal of strain is put on the sewn seam in upholstery work, so a strong thread is necessary. Check the tension of the thread. When you use thick materials the tension adjuster will need altering; slack thread will allow seams to 'grin' (open) and show the thread, giving a bad seam.

The needle gauge is important and the gauge used depends upon the type of fabric being machined. The following gauges are suitable for the machining of various types of covering encountered in upholstery work.

Gauge 14   Calico, light woollen fabric, silk
Gauge 16   Heavy calico (duck) thick woollen fabric
Gauge 18/19   Heavy woollen tweed, thick cotton tapestry, hessian

Leather and simulated leather   Machining of leather, or simulated leather, is generally more difficult and involves more problems than the machining of soft coverings. A good deal more practice is required to produce perfect work when working with either of these two types of coverings; these materials are dealt with later in this section.

Piping

Piping is a method of concealing and strengthening seams of cushions and other parts of the covering. Contemporary upholstery designers use far less piping as a feature of the work that was once the case, preferring to leave seams visible in order to attain a sleeker or less fussy appearance.

When piping is incorporated in the finishing or tailoring of the covering it should be cut from a strip of fabric, preferably on the bias of the weave (at 45°), approximately 30 mm (1¼ in) wide. The cord machined within the strip of fabric to form the body of the piping should be proper piping cord which is a soft, white, very pliable cord obtainable in different thicknesses. The thicknesses suitable for upholstery use are No. 1 (fine), No. 2 (medium), and No. 3 (thick and bulky). No. 2 is the most popular size and is suitable for most types of work.

In making up and machining the piping, a piping foot should be used; if one is not available, a one-sided zipper foot will be a good substitute. It is impossible to machine piping with an ordinary flat seaming foot. A one-sided foot is particularly useful when machining piping being made from velvet covering, escpecially if it is thick

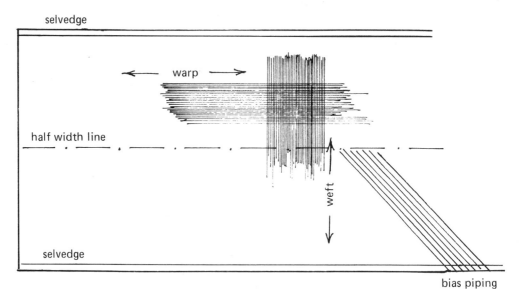

selvedge

warp

half width line

weft

selvedge

bias piping

Diagram 28
The angle at which the fabric for bias piping should be cut

Diagram 29
Sewing machine pressure foot for flat seaming

Diagram 30
Sewing machine pressure foot for piping or welting

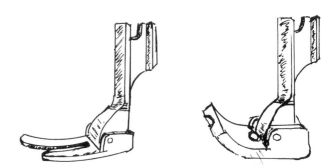

velvet, as it will not mark the velvet while this is passing between the pressure foot and feed teeth.

When made up the flange of the piping should be equal to the seaming allowance given on the main covering; this should be about 10 mm (⅜ in) wide. Always give the same allowance throughout for all seams; never over-cut sizes with the idea of trimming off the surplus after machining: accurate finished sizes will never be attained that way.

Diagram 31
When machine sewing piping, the seam allowance and the flange of the piping should be the same width, 1 cm (⅜ in)

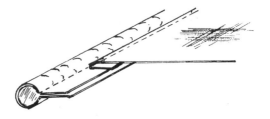

Pleating corners

There are various methods of neatly fixing and finishing the covering at the corners of seats and backs, etc. It is essential that the cut edges of the fabric and any loose yarn are hidden under the fold and that the

72

Diagram 32
Folding the covering on a square corner: (a) fold and tack the fabric, (b) cut the excess material away

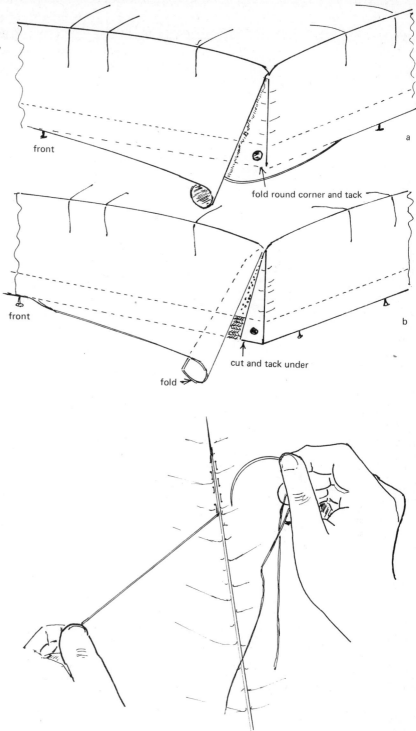

front

fold round corner and tack

a

front

cut and tack under

fold

b

Diagram 33
Slip-stitching with the circular needle and strong thread to close the covering; the thread should be pulled tight after every three or four stitches

fold remains tightly in position preventing the filling from being exposed when the seat or back is compressed. The fold of the pleat should be arranged so that from the front view one does not look *into* the fold but *on* it. Diagram 32 shows stages in forming a pleat on

73

the corner of a small seat with a foam filling. If the pleat is longer with deeper filling the fold should be 'slip stitched' to close it completely; this will prevent any exposure of the interior when the panel is compressed.

For corners which have a slight radius, double pleats (two folds) are more suitable. The folds in this case should face each other. Larger radius corners look neater with a number of smaller pleats (termed fan pleating).

Diagram 34
Pleating for rounded corners: (a) double pleating on a slight radius corner, (b) fan pleating on a larger radius corner

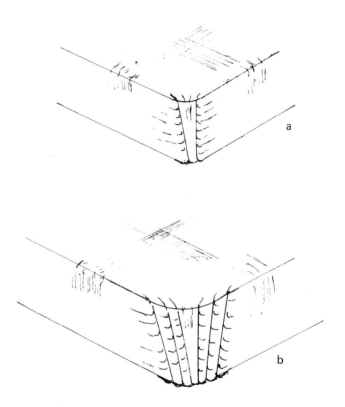

Fitting round stiles

When the covering has been prepared for fitting on to the upholstery and laid upon the surface of the filling 'stiles' (parts of the timber frame) will frequently obstruct the covering in two or three places when you try to tuck it down the sides of the filling. The covering will have to be cut around these obstructions very carefully so that the covering may be tucked into position on the appropriate rails.

To ensure that the covering will not fray and show ragged threads around the stiles after cutting or some time after, or be over-cut allowing the filling to be exposed, a great deal of care should be taken and thought given to the best method of cutting the covering around the stile. Diagrams 35-37 show typical stiles frequently encountered and suitable methods of cutting covering around them to achieve a snug fit.

In all cases it is important that prior to cutting around a stile the covering be held in position by temporary tacking or temporary

74

Diagram 35
Making a diagonal cut in the covering
fabric at the corner stile of a dining
chair

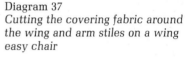

Diagram 36
Making a forked cut in the covering
fabric around the arm stile on a
fireside chair

Diagram 37
Cutting the covering fabric around
the wing and arm stiles on a wing
easy chair

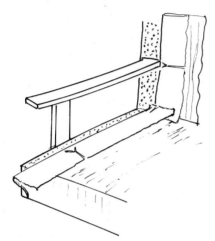

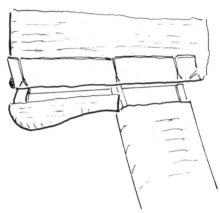

stapling, that is, hammering a tack only halfway home so that it may
be removed easily or, in the case of staples, holding the staple gun
slightly off the surface being covered so that the staple will only go
partway in. Should the cut made around the stile not be quite
accurate it is then a fairly simple matter to adjust the positioning of
the covering to put it right without your having to remove fully
embedded tacks or staples. Any covering, whether it be a top
covering or undercovering in any form, should be held in position in
the first instance only by temporary tacking.

Leather and PVC-coated fabrics

Leather has enjoyed popularity as an upholstery covering fabric over
very many years. It is acceptable in any sort of situation; in the
boardroom, in the office or in the home; it will give the person living
with it a sense of luxury and well-being. Unfortunately, over recent
years, as with most luxury products, the cost of leather has risen
considerably, encouraging substitutes or simulated leather coverings
to take its place. Leather has held its ground, however, and is still
being used for upholstery a great deal. Although the graining and
colouring of modern simulated leathers are very near the real thing,
the feel and odour of real leather can not be reproduced.

Cowhide is the usual skin used for upholstery covering with other skins, such as morocco (goatskin) and roan (sheepskin) used occasionally. These are much smaller, more expensive and more difficult to work with.

An average size cowhide would be approximately 4.5 to 4.7 sq m (48 to 50 sq ft)—cowhide is sold by the square measurement and not lineal measurement as is PVC. Larger and smaller skins are available depending upon your requirements and upon availability. Curriers (processors of cowhides) do not generally supply smaller quantities than half skins (cut down the backbone) owing to the difficulty of disposing of the remainder of a cut skin. Smaller off-cuts for small items of upholstery are sometimes available from a source using leather for some manufacturing process which is glad of an outlet for its scraps.

Diagram 38
Shape and approximate measurements of a cowhide supplied for upholstery purposes

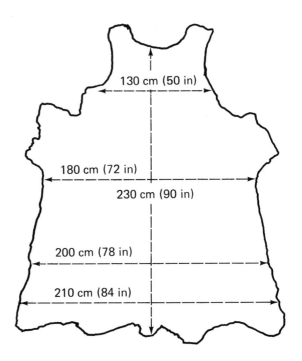

130 cm (50 in)

180 cm (72 in)

230 cm (90 in)

200 cm (78 in)

210 cm (84 in)

For reasons of economy other materials such as linen, calico or even hessian are sometimes sewn on to the leather to serve as extension pieces where part of the covering will not actually be visible. These extension pieces are known as 'flys' and the use of these is a legitimate method of saving on any type of covering.

Modern upholstery leathers are beautifully soft, some as soft as fabric and as easy to work with, with more usable leather per skin than the hides processed years ago. However, due to the uneven shape of a cowhide with its ragged outline, some of which cannot be used, cutting does present more difficulties than the cutting of fabric. To avoid errors in the cutting of such expensive material it is advisable to make templates for each piece of hide to be cut.

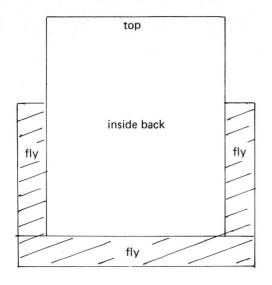

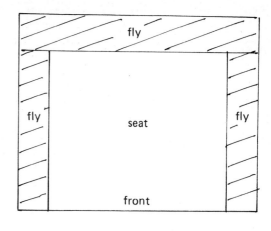

Diagram 39
A fly made of hessian can be sewn to the seat and back to economise on the covering material

Estimating quantities In estimating the quantity of leather required for a particular item it must be remembered that there is invariably a percentage of waste due to the templates not fitting exactly into the shape of the skin. To assess the amount of leather required, the net areas of every template should be added together and a percentage added to this total for wastage. Small size cuts of leather will, of course, be easier to cut with less waste than larger cuts. An average amount of waste percentage to add to the net size to arrive at the total amount required would be 20 per cent extra for small cuts, with 25 to 30 per cent for larger cuts. Failure to add this waste allowance to net sizes will mean that you will not have enough leather to complete the work.

Machining The machining of leather and PVC in preparation for upholstery covering is rather more difficult than the machining of soft fabric covers. Extra care is needed so that a line of machining is not done in error and has to be altered and re-done. A line of machine needle holes will invariably disappear when the stitches are removed from a fabric but this is unfortunately not true with leather and PVC. They will remain and rather spoil the look of the item.

The stitch length used when working on leather should be greater than the length of stitch used for fabric. For leather machining there should be approximately 3 to 4 stitches per cm (8 to 10 per in). Close needle perforations in leather will greatly weaken a seam and possibly cause splitting along a seam if it is tensioned tightly, particularly across the seam; this may happen some time after the upholstering.

Unsupported PVC (unbacked plastic sheet) should also be stitched with large stitches as it is even more prone to splitting than leather. Expanded PVC is less liable to seam splitting thanks to its knitted backing of cotton yarn; this reinforces any seaming.

The Drop-in Seat

One of the secrets of good upholstery craftsmanship is the ability to manipulate fabrics to remove 'fullness' or wrinkling; for the beginner, working on a loose seat, whether repairing an old one or making a new one, is an excellent introduction to this skill.

The first requirement is a comfortable working bench. The professional in his workshop will have a pair of trestles readily available with a board to lay across them, for the amateur an old table may be used. Don't use a good table; in stripping off the old upholstery there will be a fair amount of movement of the seat being worked upon which is likely to damage a polished surface. In any case, a polished surface will mean that the seat will just skid around even more.

Removing old tacks and staples

A ripping chisel and mallet would normally be used to remove the old tacks; if these tools are not available, an old screwdriver and cabinet hammer will be suitable substitutes. The old tacks should be removed by placing the blade of the chisel against the head of the tack which is generally protruding slightly, then sharply tapping the chisel in the direction of the wood grain: two or three sharp taps with the mallet will normally be sufficient.

On no account remove the tacks across the grain of the wood as this will invariably result in part of the timber frame breaking off, causing extra work in repairs to the frame. This applies particularly to corners; always work inwards from each corner.

In some instances staples may have been used to fix the covering in position. These may be lifted by using a staple extractor or a long pointed instrument, such as an upholsterer's regulator, which may be forced under the crown or bridge of the staple to raise it slightly after which it may be removed easily with a pair of pincers or pliers.

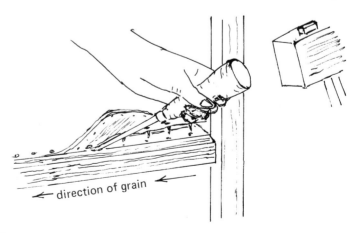

Diagram 40
A ripping chisel and mallet are used to remove old tacks when stripping covering; tacks must be removed along the grain of the timber to avoid damaging it

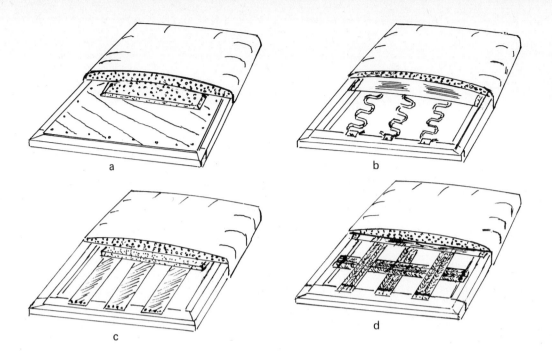

a

b

c

d

Diagram 41

Upholstery of loose 'drop in' seats: (a) foam on plywood or hardboard, (b) foam on serpentine springing with hessian (burlap) over, (c) foam on rubber webbing, (d) foam on linen or jute webbing with hessian over

Webbing   The diagrams show various methods of upholstering a loose seat. If the supporting base is plywood or hardboard and this has been damaged and is unserviceable, it may be replaced with the same type of support using new boards or, alternatively, may be replaced with the traditional type of jute or linen webbing; this will result in a less unyielding base and give a better result. Rubber webbing is not generally suitable for a small area such as the average loose seat. If the original suspension of the seat was serpentine or sinuous springing and one or more of the springs are unserviceable, again these may be replaced with webbing.

Foam   It will be noted that an insert of an extra piece of 1.2 cm (½ in) foam has been laid over the ply base; this ensures that the seat will have a domed appearance when the main piece of foam is laid over this. The insert piece should be cut smaller than the main piece of foam as shown and should have the edges chamfered. To do this, trim the insert with a pair of scissors so that there is a 'feathered' edge all round; the chamfered edge should then be laid on to the base rather than be on the upper surface. This chamfering will avoid a sudden change in thickness which would be apparent when the seat is covered. It is also an advantage to chamfer the edges of the main foam, again placing the foam chamfered side down on the base.

   If the foam is being placed upon a ply or hardboard base, a 5 cm (2 in) wide line of contact adhesive should be applied to both the underside of the foam and to the base; this is to make sure that the foam will not shift from position.

Hessian   A base of webbing or serpentine springs should have a covering of hessian (burlap) tacked over to prevent the foam being

79

forced through the gaps between the webs or springs; adhesive can be used as described above to hold the foam in position on the hessian.

Undercover The outer covering may, if desired, be applied immediately over the foam but a far better result will be achieved if an undercovering of thin calico or a lining of some kind is used to cover the foam first, particularly if latex foam is being used (as mentioned earlier, light filtering through a top covering tends to shorten the life of latex foam considerably). Further benefits are that the desired shape can be obtained first with the calico and that the top covering will not be gripped by the foam if there is an insulating material between.

Fitting the seat Having prepared the seat for covering, test the fit of the seat into the rebate of the chair using a cutting of the actual fabric the seat is to be covered with. If you hold two thicknesses of the fabric over the rebate and gently press the seat into position so that the fabric is clamped between the seat frame and the chair frame, the seat should slide into position with gentle pressure but without forcing. On no account should the seat be hammered in; doing this will open the joints in the chair frame causing extra work in repairs.

If the seat is being re-covered with a fabric thinner than the original one it may be necessary to adjust the fit by adding a strip or two of cardboard to fill up any gap left between seat and chair frame. The cardboard should be tacked or stapled on to the edges of the seat frame as necessary.

Should the covering be a good deal thicker than the original, it may be necessary to plane or rasp a small amount off one or more of the edges of the frame before fitting either the calico undercovering or the top covering. Working with a new seat frame and chair this fitting operation should be undertaken at the commencement of upholstery.

Covering the seat Having established that there will be no problem with fitting the seat using the fabric we have chosen, the fabric should be placed in position on the seat and fixed by temporary tacking only on the *underside* of the frame using 10 mm (⅜ in) or 12 mm (½ in) tacks or staples fixed partly home only. Covering of upholstery should always be temporarily tacked only in the first instance as this allows for easy adjustment of the covering if it is found to be incorrectly positioned. It is not easy to remove tacks or staples that have been driven home and misplaced coverings, especially if there is a striped effect, will mar the final appearance of the work. Patience at this stage will have its just reward.

Centre the covering on the seat along the front and back edges. It is a simple matter to make a pencil or chalk mark at the centre of the frame (on the underside) and also to notch or mark the centre of the covering so that when it is positioned these marks may be aligned. The weave of fabric from side to side should run parallel with the front edge of the seat frame.

Diagram 42
Tensioning the cover to remove fullness or wrinkling

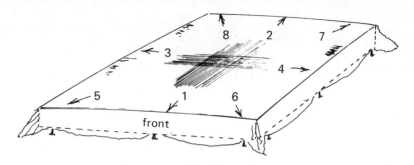

During the temporary tacking process, while you are checking the straight-lay of the covering, any wrinkles should be smoothed away by gently tensioning the fabric diagonally into the corners. Care should be taken to avoid 'tack ties', that is, tensioning too tightly at one particular point so that the position of the tacks or staples is apparent over the top of the seat where the weave of the fabric is distorted. Should this happen the fixing of the covering at that point should be removed and the covering re-tacked slightly looser.

Having established that the covering is positioned and tensioned satisfactorily, a permanent fixing can now be effected by hammering home 10 mm (⅜ in) fine tacks or staples, progressively easing out the temporary tacks or staples as you work along the front, back and two sides (in that order).

Care should be taken with folding (pleating) the covering at the corners, diagram 32 shows the sequence of tacking, cutting away surplus and folding the material to prevent having a bulky corner which may prevent the seat fitting into the chair rebate.

Neatening The underside of the seat may be neatened by tacking a piece of calico, linen or similar cloth over the base, finishing about 10 to 12 mm (⅜ to ½ in) in from the outer edges of the frame. The raw edges of this bottoming should be folded under and tacked with 10 mm (⅜ in) fine tacks or be stapled. The tacks or staples should be put in right on the edge of the fold to prevent the edges rolling back.

An alternative method of finishing the covering on the underside, which may be a little more difficult for the inexperienced, is to turn the edges of the top covering under as it is being tacked on to the underside of the frame. This will get rid of the raw edges of the top fabric so that a bottom covering need not be applied (assuming the rest of the work on the base of the seat is presentable).

Stools

The construction and upholstery of a stool is a relatively simple exercise for a beginner. A stool may be made in a number of ways, depending upon the worker's woodworking ability, especially when working with a hard timber such as beech which is the timber normally used for upholstery frame-making.

To construct a timber chair frame to be upholstered a number of woodworking tools are of course needed and in addition sash and 'G' cramps are required to pull the joints together. Joints normally used for upholstery frames are dowelled, using 10 mm (⅜ in) grooved dowels, one, two or three dowels per joint depending upon the thickness of timber being used. To persuade the dowels to enter the dowel holes and to ensure a tight joint requires the aid of a cramp. For anyone working with upholstery a sash cramp is a wise buy.

A simple stool frame needing very little woodworking ability and a minimum number of tools and having simple upholstery is shown in diagram 43. The frame should be constructed from hardwood, such as beech or similar timber, with the side members being screwed together instead of the normal method of dowelling.

To strengthen the joints corner braces are screwed to the insides of the corners fitting flush with the lower edges of the side rails; this will enable steel plates to be screwed on the base corners into which legs can be screwed. These legs and fixing plates are readily obtainable at most DIY stores.

Diagram 43
Construction of a simple stool

Webbing Resilient rubber webbing may be used to support the foam filling, the webbing being secured to the top edges of the two long side members in one direction only. Four strands of 50 mm (2 in) or five strands of 36 mm (1½ in) webbing should be used and tacked with 12 mm (½ in) fine tacks or 10 mm (⅜ in) staples. Each strand of webbing should be tensioned equally using a tension of between 7½ and 10 per cent. The method of ensuring attaining an equal tension on each strand is shown in plates 26 and 27, with the webbing fixed on the two long members. Rather than cut four or five lengths off the roll separately, the two ends of the roll should be used and fixed in position simultaneously and then trimmed so there is no wastage.

After tacking or stapling the first edge of webbing, lay the web across to the opposite side and mark with pencil or biro the position on the web where the inner line of the frame member comes. Then when the web is tensioned the amount of elongation is apparent; this should be approximately 18 to 25 mm (¾ to 1 in). For a seat of this size it is unnecessary to apply webbing in both directions. The webbing should not be folded over at the tacking points as is usual with jute or linen webbing.

Applying foam The foam interior should now be cut. A suitable thickness for this stool might be 5 cm (2 in) of a fairly firm density. With a small stool such as this it is unnecessary to cut a template as a guide for cutting the foam; the stool frame should be light enough to turn upside down and lay on the foam so that the size of the top may be marked around the edges with a felt tip pen. The foam should then be cut to the outside of this marking; this will give the slight amount of oversize cut necessary for a satisfactory fit, bearing in mind that foam tends to reduce slightly in size while being worked and covered.

The foam must be cut with perfectly upright and square sides. If you are cutting with some sort of hand knife this should be held perfectly straight while you are cutting; ragged edges should be avoided (plates 9, 10 and 29). As mentioned earlier, cut with long firm strokes upwards rather than with a sawing action.

A flange for fixing the foam should now be stuck to the cut edges on all four sides. This may be made from calico or some similar material and should be stuck halfway up the sides of the foam leaving a loose flap for stapling or tacking to the frame. This operation will prevent the foam from moving laterally after the covering has been applied. 10 mm (⅜ in) fine tacks or staples are suitable for securing the flanges to the sides of the frame.

Diagram 44
Fixing the foam to the frame

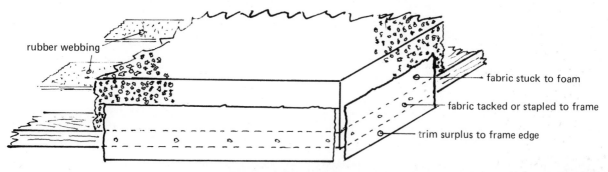

rubber webbing

fabric stuck to foam

fabric tacked or stapled to frame

trim surplus to frame edge

Covering The fabric cutting size for the covering should be checked at this stage; 18 to 25 cm (¾ to 1 in) on all four sides should be sufficient to secure the covering on the underside of the frame so this amount should be added to the measurement from the lower edges of the frame over the foam in both directions.

To ensure that the covering is being put on straight and square it should be temporarily fixed with tacks or staples on the underside, being permanently fixed only when you are satisfied with its positioning. The method of cutting and pleating the corners is shown in diagram 32; as the compression of the foam would cause the corners to 'gape' open, these should be neatly slip-stitched (diagram 33).

An alternative to the slip-stitching method is to 'tailor' the corners, that is, to cut the fabric at the four corners allowing sufficient for a seam of 10 mm (⅜ in) and to pin the edges together so they may be machined. The covering should be left temporary tacked only while the tailoring is being undertaken, then removed for machining. Although this is a longer procedure, the tailored corner is much neater.

The covering may be finished off on the underside by leaving the covering with a raw edge after trimming away any surplus, and then applying a lining or calico bottom, or by turning the raw edges under neatly so that bottoming is unnecessary.

A period stool

A period stool has a simplified frame construction involving no jointing of timber; it requires few tools and little frame-making skill. The base support for the foam may be chipboard or plywood with beech cabriole legs screwed to the four corners. With prudent selection of suitable covering material and trimming the stool could

42 A period style stool upholstered with foam, braid trimming being glued around the base of the seat

blend in well in a period setting, although made and upholstered using modern techniques.

The chipboard or plywood should be of a thickness of about 20 to 22 mm (¾ in). The cabriole legs may be purchased at many DIY stores in the 'white', in sets of four at different heights; a suitable height for this particular stool would be 230 to 305 mm (9 to 12 in).

A suitable size for the base would be 45 cm (1 ft 6 in) square. When the baseboard has been cut to the desired size, the shape of the tops of the cabriole legs should be outlined on each of the four corners of the baseboard where they are to be attached. Five screw hole positions should be marked within each outline (plate 43) and holes drilled to take 7 gauge screws 50 mm (2 in) long. To ensure accuracy a card template may be made of the leg top with suitable screw positions marked by making a hole through the card so that a pencil can be used to reproduce the drilling positions through the holes on to the base. This preparation for drilling needs to be done with accuracy as the screw holes in legs and base must line up.

The screws should first be partly screwed into the base to get

43 Drilling holes in the baseboard of the stool for screwing on the cabriole legs

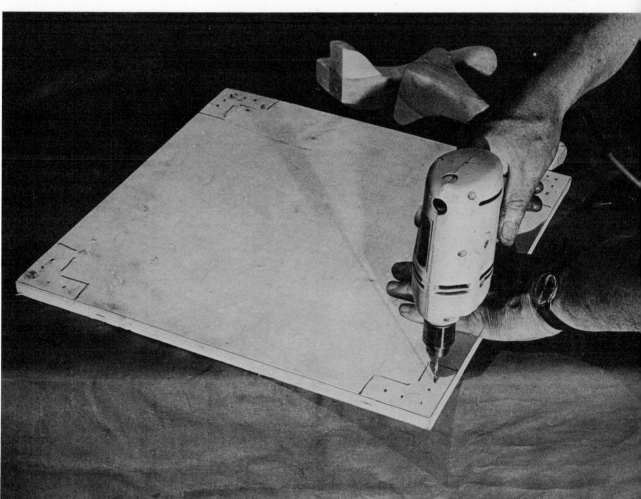

started, then, with the leg correctly positioned underneath, screwed home. In the absence of a bench vice to hold the legs firm while screwing, a helping hand to steady the base and legs will make the job easier.

Foam interior and covering The foam interior of either polyether or latex should be marked out for size using the base laid upon the surface of the foam as a guide. Draw a line around the outer edge of the base with a felt tip pen.

When cutting the foam make the cut on the outside of the marked line so that it remains on the foam you have cut; this will ensure that the foam is fractionally oversize, say 3 mm (⅛ in) all round. Take care to make the cuts perfectly upright and square if cutting manually with a knife.

Two methods of fixing the foam to the base may be used:

(a) applying adhesive to the surface of the baseboard and to one surface of the foam and carefully placing them together so that the slight 'oversize' is equal all round. The adhesive need only be in a band approximately 5 to 7.5 cm (2 to 3 in) from the outer edges.

(b) sticking a strip of calico or some such material to the edges of the foam about half way up the side edges, leaving a flange to be tacked or stapled to the edges of the baseboard. This method, if used, makes for easier removal of the foam at a later date when it may need replacing as it avoids having to tear the foam off the board as when it is stuck to the board.

An undercovering of calico may be fitted before the top covering is applied the undercovering being fixed in position on the outside edge of the base. An undercovering is certainly advisable if latex foam is being used.

The 'pullover' edge If the 'pullover' type of finish for the covering is to be used, the measurement for the covering should be taken from one bottom edge up the side, across the top and down the opposite side adding approximately 25 mm (1 in) on each side for fixing the covering under the base. When applying the covering place it in position by tempory tacking or stapling in the first instance to check on the straightness of the weave and of any pattern the fabric may have, fixing permanently only when you have done this. Where the legs meet the baseboard the covering will be tacked or stapled to the edge of the board, the fixing being hidden by a braid or gimp attached all round the base.

A trimmed edge A trimmed edge finish is more difficult than the 'pullover' style of finish described above and involves absolutely accurate cutting and machining of the covering.

The trimming used for this style would normally be ruche but piping may be used if a less decorative or fussy appearance is required. Piping may also be more suitable if a plainer style of leg is being used.

86

To achieve a good appearance the top panel and side borders of the covering must be tailored accurately with the cut edges parallel with the weave of the fabric. This is indeed important in any cutting operation; fabric cut off the weave (or grain as it is sometimes referred to) will not set correctly during machining nor will it lay right on any foam surface. If piping is to be used, this should be cut on the bias of the weave rather than be cut straight across the width.

When cutting the top panel for a flat surfaced stool an allowance of 10 mm (⅜ in) for seaming should be given over the finished size on all four sides. An equal amount of seaming allowance should be made along the top edge of the side borders (these borders should be joined at the four corners where the same seaming allowance is necessary). The cutting depth of the side borders should be the foam and base depth plus the seaming allowance along the top edge plus 25 mm (1 in) for fixing the border to the underside of the stool base.

A slightly domed top surface, generally more desirable for a period style than a flat one, will require an additional allowance over the normal seaming allowance to allow for the greater distance over the domed area than along the straight edges. If this extra amount of covering is not given, the edges will turn out to be concave rather than straight (referred to as 'dog eared' corners).

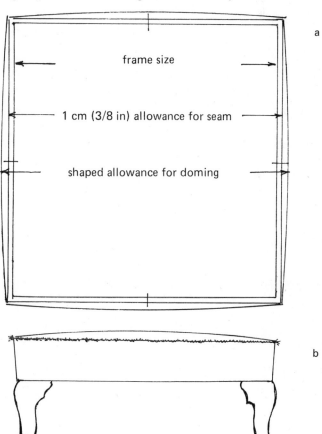

frame size

1 cm (3/8 in) allowance for seam

shaped allowance for doming

a

b

Diagram 45
Shaping the top panel of the seat cover to give a domed appearance: (a) the seaming and doming allowance, (b) amount of doming suitable

When placing the machined covering over the foam-covered base it is again important to temporary tack or staple the covering into position. Use should be made of a rule or tape measure to measure the depth of the finished side borders to ensure that all four sides are of an equal depth before tacks or staples are driven home.

The flange of the ruched or piped seam should lay *down* the side borders towards the bottom edge of the stool. As the covering is being eased into position put your hand inside it to smooth the flange down to the correct position. If it is allowed to lie partly on the top of the foam and partly down the side the result will be an uneven edge giving an unsightly appearance, which will also wear badly.

Finishing off   The underside of the base should be covered neatly with black linen, calico or hessian using 10 mm (⅜ in) fine tacks or 6 mm (¼ in) staples for fixing. If cabriole legs have been used, the bottoming needs careful cutting around the shape which is fixed to the baseboard.

Diagram 46
Cutting and tailoring the bottom covering to fit round the base of a cabriole leg

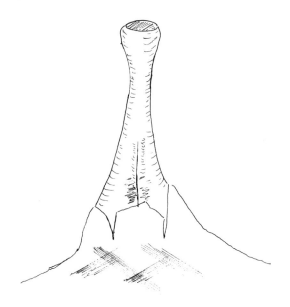

The Box Pouffe

This is an excellent exercise to learn the intricate art of upholstery buttoning using foam rather than the traditional fillings of fibre and hair. The basic box is made from chipboard or plywood and is fairly simple to put together, the sides being screwed together and covered before the base is fixed and the top upholstered.

There are two methods of using upholstery buttons whether simply for decorative purposes or as an aid in procuring or retaining the shape of a particular section of an upholstered piece. The primary use of buttoning in either case is to help to control the covering material and to take away unsightly fullness or wrinkling of the covering.

The simplest form of buttoned work is known as 'float' buttoning. Apart from marking the positions of the buttons on the surface of the covering after it has been fixed in position, very little preparation work is necessary. The buttons are sewn through both the covering and the upholstery filling and tied off so that they are slightly recessed into the fabric. The rather more difficult method is deep diamond pleated buttoning and this requires accurate planning and measuring and, above all, patience.

44 Float-buttoned box pouffe

Diagram 47
Construction of a box pouffe frame:
(a) exploded view of the box and lid,
(b) interior with retaining chain, (c)
float buttoned top with a machined
diamond design

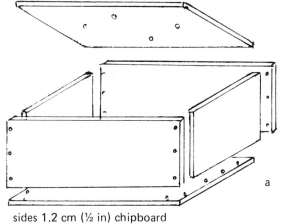

a

sides 1.2 cm (½ in) chipboard

top and base 1.6 cm (5/8 in) chipboard

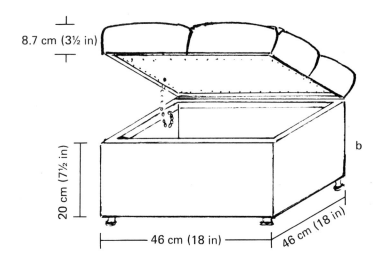

8.7 cm (3½ in)

20 cm (7½ in)

46 cm (18 in)

46 cm (18 in)

b

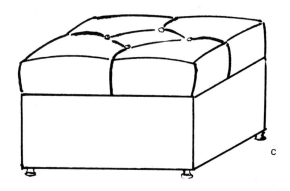

c

The buttons   The normal size upholstery button, known as size 24 or 26 (UK) will be approximately 16 mm (⅝ in) in diameter depending upon the thickness of the covering fabric, size 26 being fractionally larger than 24. The back or base of the button will have either a wire loop or a cotton fabric tuft for fixing the button in position with twine. Of the two types, the cotton tufted one is the better because the tuft will allow the button to lie completely flat on the covering whereas the wire loop frequently prevents the button bedding down properly, particularly in the case of leather or PVC coverings.

Diagram 48 shows other forms of fixing devices for upholstery buttons but these are really for specialist applications.

The making of upholstery buttons is a simple operation if you have the special cutter, dies and presses. However, the amateur (and frequently the small professional upholstery) will not usually have this equipment and will be compelled to have the buttons made through a local supplier dealing in that sort of commodity.

There is a proprietary brand of DIY button which can be made easily using your own fabric but while these are very convenient and useful they are not generally strong enough to stand the strain of tensioning with twine into the deep diamond button positions, especially if you are using a thick fabric or leather or simulated leather. It can prove very frustrating to have buttons come apart after all the preparation work you have done prior to pulling them down.

Diagram 48
Various types of button fixings for upholstery work

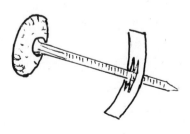

45 Hand press for cutting fabric
circles for button making

46 Hand press for forming buttons

45 Hand press for cutting fabric
circles for button making

48 A foot treadle button press

47 Cutter and dies for the hand
presses for upholstery button making

Construction and covering   An exploded view of the box is shown with the positions of the holes drilled to accept the screws. The holes should be countersunk so that the heads of the screws do not stand proud of the surface. The sides only should be screwed together in the first instance so that they may be lined with a material to match the outer covering before the base and lid are fixed in position. The inner lining should be tacked or stapled in four separate pieces with the joins in each corner; these should be folded under and slip-stitched.

Tack or staple the lining along the top inside edge of the sides without a fold and take it down to the base and fix it to the underside edges, again without a fold. At this stage the inner corners should be slip-stitched. The lining across the base should now be applied, being stretched across and tacked or stapled over the edges in the same positions as the side linings, i.e. the bottom edges. The base of the box may then be screwed into position.

To give the lining of both sides and base a softer feel a layer of skin wadding may be laid under it before the base is fixed down.

The outer covering may now be tacked or stapled on to the base. It should be 'back-tacked' along the top inner edge. By cutting the 'back-tacking' card 12 mm (½ in) wide and using this width as a guide level with the inner top edge, staple or tack the covering under it so that after fixing the card the covering may be brought over the top edges of the box and down the sides fixing under the base. The folds on corner edges should be mitred.

Wadding or felt, perhaps a little thicker than that used under the inner lining, may again be used to pad the outer surfaces.

49 The finish on the inside of the box

The outer corners of the box covering may now be slip-stitched if a soft fabric is being used. If leather or simulated leather (expanded PVC) is the covering it is rather more difficult to slip-stitch so brass, oxidised upholstery nails or covered studs may be used. The covering for the box bottom can now be put on, using a material similar to the inner lining.

Float buttoning   The buttons on the top of the box have been placed to make one large diamond with holes drilled in the lid where the buttons are to be positioned to allow the twine to hold the buttons in place to pass through.

The lines between the buttons forming the diamond shape and the lines radiating from the buttons towards the outer edges of the lid are made by cutting the covering material to these shapes (not forgetting to allow extra for seaming and for fixing under the bottom edges of the lid) and then machining the pieces together.

The foam to be used for the lid should be of a density and thickness which will not 'bottom' on to the board. The thickness should be a *minimum* of 62 mm (2½ in), preferably deeper.

While a single layer of firm foam would be reasonably satisfactory for padding the lid, a far better result will be obtained by laminating two different densities and thicknesses. For instance, if the total depth of the foam is to be 7.5 cm (3 in) a suitable combination might be a very firm foam of 62 mm (2½ in) cut to the size of the chipboard or ply and an overlay of a softer foam 12 mm (½ in) thick. The overlaid piece may be 25 mm (1 in) if extra softness is desired.

The overlay of soft foam should be placed on the firm piece and wrapped down the sides to the bottom edge. Adhesive around the outer sides will hold the overlay in place. The corners of the outer (soft) foam should be tailored, the surplus being cut away and the corner edges butted and stuck together to prevent any unevenness showing through the covering.

To attain the effect shown in fig. 39c the diamond shape and lines

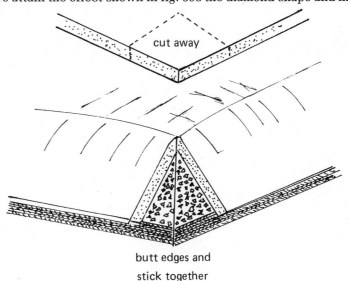

cut away

butt edges and
stick together

Diagram 49
Cutting away the surplus foam at the corners and butting the edges together to give a smooth finish

radiating from each point should be drawn on the foam, transferring the shapes on to the covering by means of templates which may include the seaming allowance.

Make sure that if fabric is being used the weave of the fabric is lined up. It is advisable to draw lines on the templates in the direction the weave should be so that they may be placed on the fabric correctly. If expanded PVC or leather is being used this problem does not arise.

When applying the covering to the lid over the foam, position it so that the points of the diamond are over the holes in the base and temporary tack or staple it in place while you put the buttons in position. These are sewn through the covering from the top using twine and a fine upholsterer's buttoning needle. The needle and twine are passed through both foam and board (through the holes in the board) and secured on the underside of the board with either staples or tacks. (It is advisable to use a good quality flax, upholsterer's twine or even nylon twine to avoid future breakage.)

If the upholstery buttons have a fabric tuft at the back care must be taken not to damage this when passing the needle and twine through, a bayonet type upholsterer's needle could well force the tuft out of the base of the button. For float buttoning the button should be pulled down only enough to allow it to make a slight indentation in the surface of the covering.

To finish off the upholstry of the lid the underside should be lined to cover the edges of the covering which have been tacked or stapled under. Brass hinges should be screwed in position with a tape or a piece of fine chain to prevent the lid opening too far. Glides or screw-on castors may be fixed to the base of the box to give freedom of movement over the floor.

A deep buttoned lid   The alternative method of 'deep' buttoning may be carried out on a pouffe lid instead of the float buttoning, but there is more preparation involved. The positions of the buttons or the size and shape of the diamond pleating need to be planned before the foam is fixed in position. This can all be worked out and marked with pencil or chalk on the board.

Assuming the box is a similar size to that in diagram 47, i.e. 46 cm (1ft 6 in) square, the buttons should be 15 cm (6 in) apart leaving the side buttons 7.5 cm (3 in) from the sides. By planning the positions of the buttons in this way the diamonds formed by the pleating of the covering will look balanced; the outer lines of buttons should be positioned from the sides approximately half the distance between the inner buttons. As the board is square the button positions can be the same distance apart in both directions.

With the button positions marked upon the board, holes should be drilled at these positions to enable the buttoning needle to pass through. The holes should be 6 mm (¼ in) minimum or slightly larger to avoid any difficulty in locating them or in getting the needle through.

The foam, once cut to size, should also be marked with the button

K.D. easy chair upholstered with foam and rubber webbing. Seat, back and arms as separate units.
Designed by Alan Notley. L.C.F.

*Modern swivel easy chair upholstered
with foam and rubber webbing. Tweed
covering.
Designed by Richard Curruthers. L.C.F.*

positions and holes cut in it to allow the buttons to sink in properly when pulled down by the twine.

The buttoning holes can easily be made in the foam with a cutting punch or with a piece of metal tube, such as gas piping about 15 cm (6 in) long with one end filed around the outer edge to give a sharp cutting edge; the tube should be 12 mm (½ in) in diameter. By holding the tube firmly and pressing it down hard into the foam to compress it as much as possible, then giving it two or three sharp blows with the tube held square, you will cut a hole.

If you attempt to button on to foam without making these holes, the buttons will not have a satisfactory 'sink'; when pulled down tightly the buttons will just pull down the surrounding foam spoiling the effect and prevent the pleating from forming and setting.

If any overlay of thinner, softer foam is being used over the main piece as suggested for the 'float' buttoned lid, the two pieces should be fixed together and the holes made through both at the same time.

With the foam now prepared and fixed in position by adhesive around the top edges of the board, the covering should be marked accurately with the button positions. So that the pleating will be formed into the diamond shapes an amount of 'fullness' is required. In order to attain this fullness the distance between the button positions marked on the covering should be greater than that marked on the base (or ground-work).

To give an average acceptable depth of buttoning the extra allowance between buttons marked on the covering should be 5 mm ($^3/_{16}$ in) to every 25 mm (1 in) between the buttons marked on the groundwork, e.g. if the distance *across* the diamonds on the ground-work from button to button is 15 cm (6 in), the extra pleating allowance would be 2.8 cm (1⅛ in) so the measurement on the covering should be marked as 18 cm (7⅛ in). In the case of this particular square seat the diamonds are the same size in both directions so the covering allowance would be the same.

In some instances the diamond shapes may be longer than they are wide so the cover marking should take account of that.

If the foam being used is fairly shallow it will not be possible to get a good depth to the buttoning, so the amount of fullness allowance should be reduced. A guide to assessing the amount of extra covering to allow is by holding a hand between the button positions and draping a tape measure over; the curve of the back of the hand can be varied to give a realistic measurement.

Diagram 50 shows the button positions marked on the covering. All marking should be on the reverse side of the covering using tailor's chalk which will give a fine line enabling accurate marking to be accomplished. On no account mark out the button positions on the face of the covering as tailor's chalk cannot always be removed and may leave lines, possibly across the centre of a diamond.

Using a fine upholsterer's buttoning needle and a good quality fine flax or nylon twine the buttons may be put in from the top of the covering ensuring that the needle penetrates the covering in the exact spot marked on the reverse side.

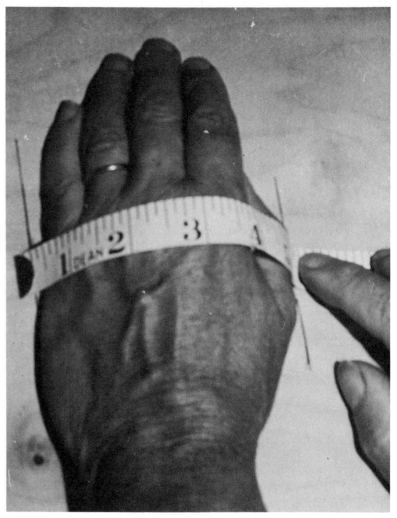

50 Assessing the amount of fullness
necessary by placing a tape measure
over the hand

Diagram 50
Marking the button positions: (a)
the baseboard of the top marked and
drilled, (b) the covering cut and
marked, including an allowance
for the diamond pleating

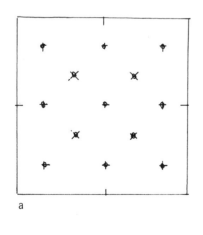

a

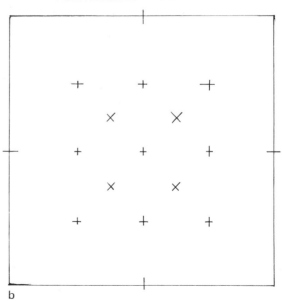

b

Start by passing the needle with a length of twine threaded in it through the back of the button (this may be a wire loop or a cotton fabric tuft), then thread the free end of the twine through the eye of the needle so that both ends are threaded. Pass the needle and twine through the covering and then through the hole in the foam. Locate the hole in the base, then pass the needle and twine right through completely.

Ease the button down lightly only, then fix the twine temporarily under the base so that an adjustment may be made when all the buttons are in position. A slip knot should be made in the twine which may be looped around a tack on the underside.

If you have any difficulty in locating the hole in the base the the process can be reversed, passing the needle and twine from the underside of the base through the foam and covering and then threading the button on to the twine. Next, with the needle free, pass the eye end through the base hole again so that it comes out of the foam and covering in the correct spot. The twine may then be threaded through the eye and pulled through the base, tensioned and fixed.

When the buttoning has been established, the sides may be tacked or stapled. Don't pull the covering too tightly as this tends to pull the pleating out of shape. The corners should be folded and pleated with the pleat slip-stitched, and the underside finished with an under-covering to match the inner lining as explained for the float buttoned box.

Diagram 51
Tying off buttons: the slip knot is suitable for holding down buttons, and they may be pulled down as deep as desired

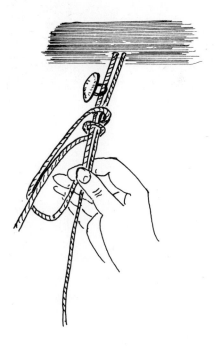

Headboards

Continuing with the art of buttoning, an ever-popular item of bedroom furnishing suitable for buttoning treatment is the bed headboard. Although deep buttoning is a traditional decoration, it is most acceptable in even the most modern decor. As the bed headboard is a flat, even surface it presents less difficulty than a curved surface or shape, such as any easy chair or settee or couch back, and is thus a suitable 'next step' for anyone who has perhaps already attempted deep buttoning, for instance on the box pouffe. The bed footboard may of course also be buttoned in a similar fashion but this seems to be less usual.)

There are many shapes which could be used for the bedhead to incorporate deep buttoning. The most usual shape is rectangular, with or without a separate border.

51 Simple headboard with float buttoning, upholstered on chipboard with 36 mm (1½ in) polyether foam; holes are drilled in the board to pass the button twines through

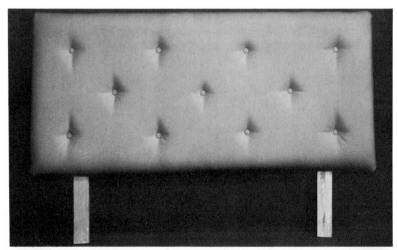

52 A headboard with a bordered surround and three large buttons inserted across the centre; it is upholstered on chipboard with 36 mm (1½ in) polyether foam in the centre panel; the border may be filled with foam, linterfelt or wadding and is back-tacked around the centre panel

A traditional-style headboard

The Queen Anne style bed headboard shown is upholstered in a 90 cm (3 ft) width. It can, of course, with adjustments to the buttoning positions, be made in a 76 cm (2 ft 6 in) width or in a greater width by increasing the distances between the buttons, or perhaps adding more of them. It is, however, a mistake in general to have too many buttons and so reduce the size of the diamonds too much; the diamond shapes formed when the buttons have been inserted and the covering pleated always tend to look smaller than they did when pencilled out on the board itself anyway. Also, having the diamond shapes too small means overcrowded buttons which spoils the effect.

53 Queen Anne style, deep diamond buttoned headboard

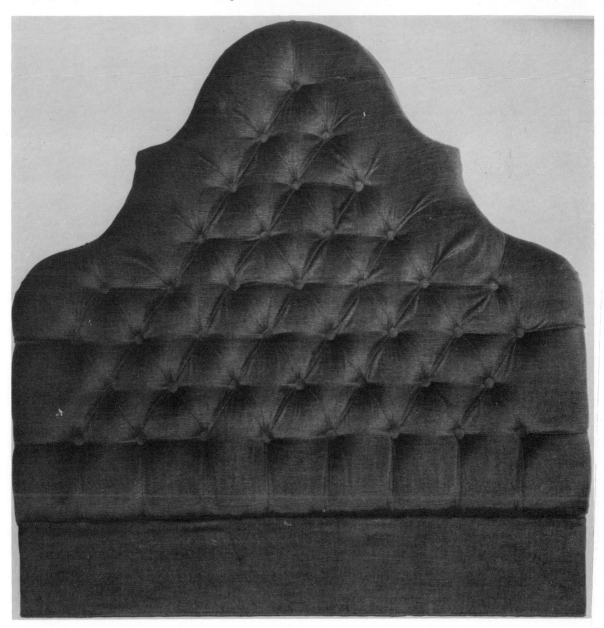

Preparation   The first requirement is the base board itself. This may be either 12 mm (½ in) plywood or a slightly thicker chipboard. Plywood is preferable because the sharp corners or edges of chipboard may flake off if it is badly handled.

The Queen Anne shape should be marked out to scale on squared paper. This can then easily be copied and marked out on the base board with a pencil using 25 mm (1 in) squares. Cut around the pencilled lines with a machine band saw or manually with a padsaw or hand electric jig saw. The pad saw will leave the cut edges somewhat rough; these should be smoothed off with coarse sandpaper before upholstery commences.

Button positions should be accurately measured and marked on the board. Using an electric or hand drill, drill the holes at these points using a 7 mm (⁵/₁₆ in) bit. Holes smaller than those produced by this size of drill bit will cause difficulties when it comes to passing the needle and twine through. Plate 51 shows the board with the holes drilled.

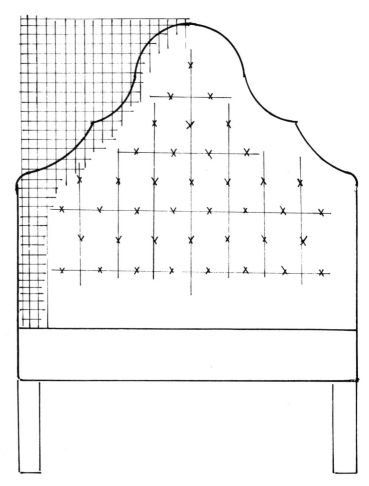

Diagram 52
Period style headboard: transfer the shape to full size using a squared grid

102

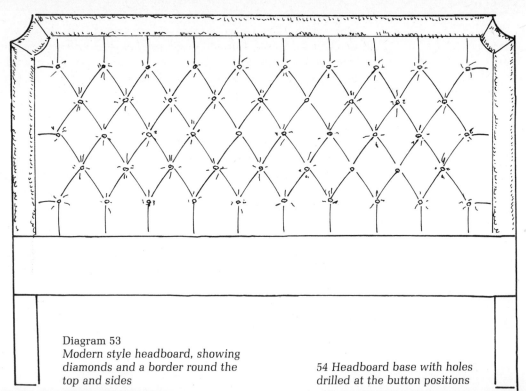

Diagram 53
Modern style headboard, showing
diamonds and a border round the
top and sides

54 Headboard base with holes
drilled at the button positions

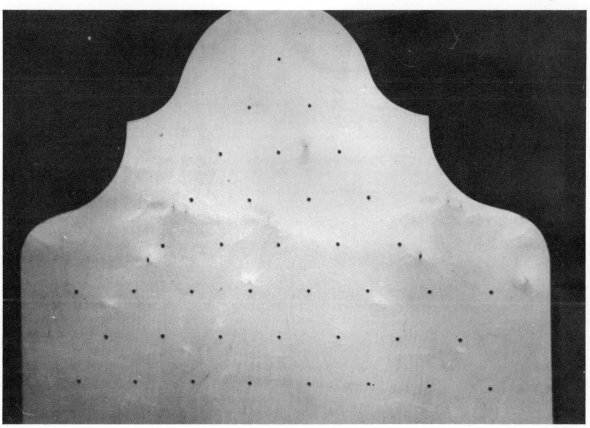

The foam   A medium density polyether foam 36 mm (1½ in) thick will be suitable for the interior padding of the headboard. The board shape already cut out may be used as a template for marking the foam: lay the board on the foam and mark around the outer edge with a felt tip pen.

The foam should be cut slightly oversize with a good, clean square edge, leaving the marked line on the foam to be used. It is an advantage to take off, by trimming with scissors, the sharp edge on the face side of the foam to give a slightly rounded edge. This also may be done with a coarse sanding disc fixed to an electric hand drill. Doing this will avoid any danger of the sharp corner edge showing through the covering, particularly if the covering is on the thin side.

The base line of the foam shape should be cut shorter than the board by 12.5 to 15 cm (5 to 6 in) so as to allow the mattress to fit tight up to the headboard underneath the bottom line of the upholstery.

The position of the holes in the base board should now be marked on the foam by laying the board on it (carefully aligned) and marking through the holes with a slim felt tip pen or biro. If the holes are too small to allow this, an easy alternative is to use some form of powder, such as French chalk or talcum powder. Dust the powder into the holes so that it drops through on to the foam. When you have, carefully, removed the board, marks may be made where the powder spots are.

12 mm (½ in) holes should be punched through the foam by the same method as described for the box pouffe lid, i.e. using a sharpened piece of metal tube as a punch. Make sure that the piece of foam punched out is actually removed from the hole.

It is not necessary for the foam to be stuck to the base in this case: the buttons as they are tied in will hold the foam firmly in position. It is advisable that two or three spare buttons be made or ordered as an insurance against breakages as one or two tufts or wire loops may come away from the cap making them unusable and having the exact number only is tempting fate!

55 Rounding the edge of the foam with an abrasion disc fitted to an electric drill

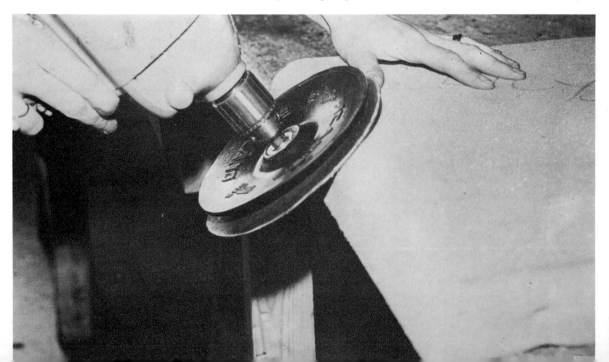

Preparing the covering   The covering should now be cut roughly to size so that the button positions may be marked on the reverse side of the material with tailor's chalk. To establish an approximate size for cutting, the measurement straight over the foam in both directions should be taken adding a suitable amount to finish on the back of the headboard.

In addition to this, the amount of fullness to give deep buttoning should be added in both directions. This can be calculated by counting the number of full diamond shapes down, then multiplying the amount of fullness by the number of diamonds or half diamonds to the 'flat' size. Do the same across also. This will tell you the extra material needed for the depth of the buttons. The procedure of working out the fullness is as explained in the section on the pouffe lid, i.e. 5 mm (^{3}/$_{16}$ in) for every 25 mm (1 in) of ground-work between the buttons.

The button positions should be marked on the covering, working from the top of the board and allowing sufficient covering with a little to spare for fixing the covering to the top outer edge. After establishing the position of the topmost button which should be dead centre of the width, the *full* diamond positions should then be marked, ignoring the intermediate rows and working down to the last of the full diamonds. Lines should be drawn with tailor's chalk across the width of the fabric, care being taken to follow the fabric weave. If these lines are drawn off the weave, the pleating forming the diamond shapes will not set. Working across the width of the fabric the full diamond shapes should then be marked on the lines running across. It is not necessary to draw complete lines all the way down but just make a cross which will be the spot at which the buttoning needle should penetrate the covering.

With the full diamonds marked in both directions, by laying the straight edge along the crossed lines, the intermediate positions can be found without measuring. Again it is not necessary to draw lines right across diagonally; short lines drawn roughly across the centres of the spaces in both directions will form crosses which will give the needle penetration spots. (Diagram 54 shows the ground marking for the more modern style headboard with a border along top and sides.)

Tying in the buttons   Before you start on the buttoning make a final check that the button positions are marked correctly on the covering. In addition, ensure that the first button inserted is in its correct position as it is possible practically to finish work such as this only to realise that the covering has been put in position one row of buttons too high or too low.

Having established the first button in its position by threading the buttoning needle and twine through the tuft or wire loop at the back of the button, thread the two ends of twine through the covering at one of the centre button positions or near the centre of the headboard and then through the hole in the foam and board. Make a slip knot (diagram 51) and hook the twine over a 10 mm (^{3}/$_8$ in) temporary tack without pulling it right down. Leave the button in this temporary

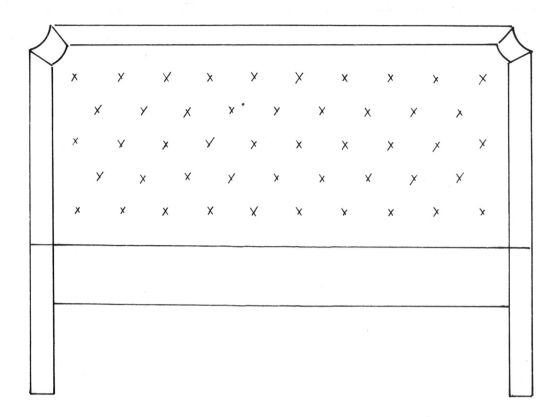

Diagram 54
Button positions marked on a full-size modern headboard

state and proceed with the others, working outwards from this first one and completing a diamond at a time.

Pleating   With the aid of the flat end of a regulator smooth the fullness into orderly pleating between the buttons so that evenly shaped diamonds are formed. The pleating may need some persuading depending upon the type of covering; some fabrics work more easily than others. Silky types tend to slip and not hold the pleats very well but in all cases patience is required to produce a satisfactory result. Every pleat should be folded downwards, being stroked down from the top to help crease the folds into permanent pleating.

Hammer the temporary tacks or staples home only after ensuring that all the buttons are set at an equal depth and the pleating is in position. As shown in plate 53 there are pleats at certain positions from some outer buttons to the sides and top of the board; these should be set as the covering is being set and fixed around the sides. There may need to be an amount of adjustment, particularly around the concave curves as the covering will need snipping to get it into the curves.

Finishing off   When the covering is set and fixed along the bottom of the foam, which should be shorter than the base as mentioned, a piece of covering or lining should be back-tacked along this line, taken underneath and finished on the reverse side bottom edge.

The back of the headboard will be rather uneven with the twines

106

*56 The back of the headboard
showing the twines held by
temporary tacks before finishing off*

finished and cut off (plate 56) so a layer of skin wadding or thin foam
should be laid over it before a lining is applied to give a neat
appearance. Covering is an unnecessary expense unless the back of
the headboard will be visible. The lining or covering should be
pinned in position and slip-stitched neatly.

Covering wider headboards

The instructions regarding the planning of deep buttoning have so far
related only to work of a size which will enable the width of the
covering to cover the width of the headboard. There are additional
problems, however, when a wider headboard, or indeed settee,
couch back or seat, needs to be buttoned but the fabric width is not
sufficiently wide. Two alternative courses of action may be followed
to overcome this problem.

The first course is to use the fabric with the width from top to bottom on a headboard or back, or back to front on a seat, and calculate the amount of fabric needed across the work (from side to side). The disadvantage of this method is that if you are using a patterned material the motif will run sideways and if velvet is being used the pile (or nap) will lie in the wrong direction (traditionally the pile of velvet should brush downwards on upholstered items). If you are using a plain fabric, however, this problem will not arise.

The alternative method is to use the Vandyking method, that is cutting and joining the fabric (with the width of the material across the work) in such a manner that the join is hidden under the zigzag folds of the pleating following the folds between the buttons. It is necessary to allow for seaming and a slight additional allowance between the button points so that the joins are *well* hidden in the folds. Diagram 55 shows how the fabric is cut and put together for joining by machining.

Diagram 55
Vandyking, showing the method of joining fabric to avoid the appearance of seams on deep buttoned work

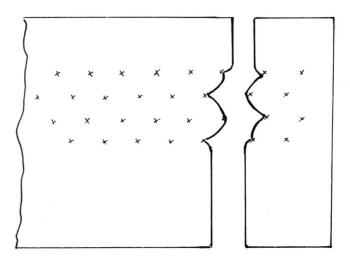

Unit Chair

This low-backed upholstered chair of sectional construction is suitable for use as an extending unit. It can form seating for two, three, four or more persons or can be made up to any length.

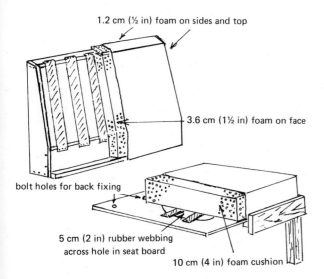

1.2 cm (½ in) foam on sides and top

3.6 cm (1½ in) foam on face

bolt holes for back fixing

5 cm (2 in) rubber webbing across hole in seat board

10 cm (4 in) foam cushion

Diagram 56
A unit chair with an upholstered back and a seat cushion; the exploded view shows the upholstery details

The frame

The framework consists of a show-wood base which may be of oak, walnut, teak or any decorative hardwood. The seat and back are separate units and fit within the base frame. The sides, back and front members of the seat frame may be made from 18 mm (¾ in) timber, 90 mm (3½ in) width; the legs, 36 mm (1½ in) square, are screwed into the inside of the corner joints. Supporting timber fillets are screwed on the inner surfaces of the sides, back and front to support the ply or chipboard to carry the seat cushion.

To give extra softness to the seat an oval hole should be cut in the supporting board across which should be tacked or stapled 4 × 2 strands of standard 50 mm (2 in) laminated rubber webbing; this section should be cut out before the board is fixed (screwed) on to the supporting fillets.

Holes should also be drilled into the seat support board to allow fixing bolts to be threaded through so that they may screw into the back frame base after upholstery of the back. The holes should be carefully lined up with matching holes in the base of the back. Circular 'T' nuts are available for the back fixing (diagram 58); these may be fixed into the holes in the base of the back to line up with the seat holes.

All sections of the frame should be finished before you attempt

109

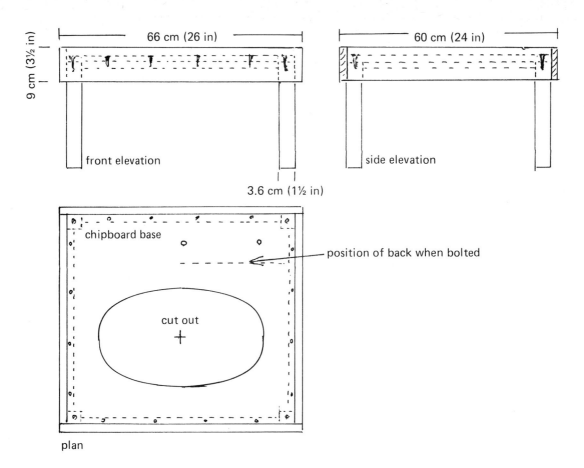

9 cm (3½ in)

66 cm (26 in)

front elevation

60 cm (24 in)

side elevation

3.6 cm (1½ in)

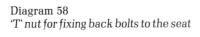

chipboard base

position of back when bolted

cut out
+

plan

Diagram 57
The seat frame construction of a unit
chair

Diagram 58
'T' nut for fixing back bolts to the seat

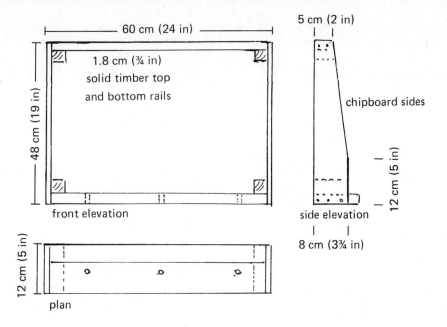

60 cm (24 in)

1.8 cm (¾ in)
solid timber top
and bottom rails

48 cm (19 in)

front elevation

12 cm (5 in)

plan

5 cm (2 in)

chipboard sides

12 cm (5 in)

side elevation

8 cm (3¾ in)

Diagram 59
The back frame construction of a unit chair

upholstering any part of it to ensure that the parts fit accurately together and the bolt holes coincide. The cross members of the back should be cut from slightly thicker hardwood than the sides so that the sides can be securely screwed into them. Chipboard may be used for the sides if desired; for added strength blocks should be glued on the inner corners (diagram 59).

The timber at the base of the back should project as far as the foam so that when the covering is tensioned at the base, it will be pulling on the firm edge of the timber and the foam will not reduce in thickness.

Hardboard or thin plywood should be pinned to the outside of the back to give reinforcement to the outside back covering; the board should be trimmed to the outside edges all round.

Upholstery materials
Upholstery of this unit is simplified by its sectional construction.

Laminated rubber webbing 5 cm (2 in) wide, approximately 5 m (16 ft 6 in)

Polyether or latex foam, firm seating density, 10 cm (4 in) thick. 61 by 46 cm (2 ft by 1 ft 6 in)

Polyether or latex foam, medium density 36 mm (1½ in) by 60 by 50 cm (2 ft by 1 ft 8 in)

Polyether or latex foam, medium density 12 mm (½ in) by 86 by 61 cm (2 ft 6 in by 2 ft)

Upholstery fabric 127 cm (50 in) wide, 1.6 m (1¾ yd)

The back

It is advisable to upholster the back section first and complete it so that the cushion can be cut and fitted after with a perfect fit.

Apply six strands of rubber webbing to the back, tacking or stapling it onto the bottom face board, tensioning it lightly (approximately 7½ per cent) and fixing it on to the top surface of the upper rail.

Cut the foam to the width of the back frame and the height from the projecting base board up to and level with the top rail.

To fix the foam in position cut strips of calico or some other thin material approximately 5 cm (2 in) wide and stick half the width of the strip along the two side edges and the bottom face edge of the foam. When dry these may be tacked or stapled to the frame so that the foam is securely held. 12 mm (½ in) foam should be laid over the outside back ply and taken round the sides of the frame. Stick the foam to the sides and also over the top; stick it to the top member and up to the face edge of the main foam over the webbing. The surplus foam at the corners should be trimmed and edges butted together. It should be unnecessary to stick the foam along the bottom of the outside back. It should *not* be taken under the bottom edge.

With the back unit thus prepared for covering, the covering can be cut and fitted (see cover cutting plan). The inside back top border and outside back can be taken over all in one piece, if desired, leaving approximately 25 to 30 mm (1 to 1¼ in) extra for fixing at both ends to

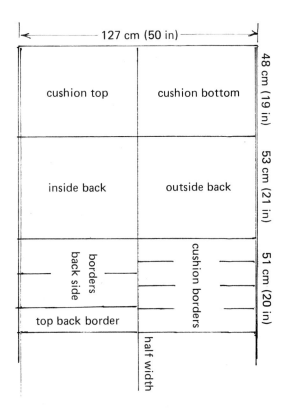

Diagram 60
Cover cutting plan for a unit chair, requiring a total amount of 1.6 m (1²/₃ yd) of fabric 127 cm (50 in) wide

112

go underneath the base of the back. The best method for cutting the side facings is to cut a template of the actual foamed-up size of the facing and cut a pair from the fabric by marking around the template with tailor's chalk and then cutting, adding the seaming allowance. The back covering should be pinned up on the reverse side and fitted before machining. An important point to pay attention to is the weave of the fabric along the top border: make sure the weave runs parallel from corner to corner.

The join between the side facings and back may be piped but will look neater and cleaner with a plain seam.

When machined, the covering should be drawn down over the foam carefully. As the covering is being eased into position the flanges of the seams should be turned so that they lie on the face of the inside and outside backs: a bad line will result if the flanges are allowed to turn in different directions.

The seat cushion

Once you have upholstered the back it should be put in position so that the actual size of the seat foam may be ascertained. This should be cut fractionally oversize to give tension to the covering when sewn. The top and bottom panels should be cut exactly the same size, with seaming allowance on the four sides, to make a reversible loose cushion. Four borders should be cut so that a join appears on each corner: the length of two borders should be the same as the length of two long edges, the other two the length of the two shorter edges.

Machine the cover, leaving an opening to insert the foam interior along a back edge. Remember, if latex foam is being used for the cushion, that an undercovering should also be made and put on before the top covering. When fitting the foam into the covering partly fold the foam to reduce its width so that the covering will slip over easily; left flat it will be impossible to get the covering over the foam with only the back edge left open. When you have filled the cushion case, close it with neat slip-stitching. When placed in position on its base the back of the cushion should fit snugly against the flat lower part of the back.

The upholstery completed, screw the bolts through the seat base into the 'T' nuts in the base of the back thus completing the unit.

Unit Armchair

This style of upholstered unit chair has a more conventional upholstered frame construction than the previous one. The arm is constructed as a separate part to be bolted to the side of the seat and back unit (optional for one or two sides). This separate arm construction will enable a number of units to be placed together with perhaps a right and left arm on each end unit only.

The frame

The framework for the body of the chair and arms is a more precise and difficult construction than that of the previous project, involving as it does cutting, drilling, dowelling, glueing and cramping of the frame members, but for the professional woodworker or keen amateur it should hold no real terrors. (Upholstery of the unit also is a little more complicated than for the earlier one but, again, it should not be too difficult following the instructions given here.)

The seat and back of the unit are combined in the one frame and made up of chipboard or plywood sides screwed to cross members of the unit which is of sold hardwood, such as beech. Diagram 64 shows construction of the unit with sizes and how the side panels are jointed to the cross members. The measurements may be increased or decreased as required. The timber should be beech if possible (planed).

The parts of the frame are as follows:

Two base front and back stretchers 45 mm (1¾ in) square

Upper front seat rail
Rear seat stretcher
Upper back rail ⎬ 50 by 25 mm (2 by 1 in)
Upper side seat members

Inner side back members 25 by 25 mm (1 by 1 in)

Side facing of 16 mm (⅝ in) chipboard with join at junction of seat and back

Hardboard back panel

Hardboard front border panel

Chipboard seat and back panels should first be cut to size and shape, working out the slope (rake) of the back desired (the angle of joining the chipboard depends upon this). The whole side panel could be cut from one piece of chipboard but this is rather wasteful; provided the join is braced strongly on the inside, the unit will be quite sound. All cross members should be cut precisely the same width taking care the cuts are square.

The chipboard can now be glued and screwed to the cross members using a good length screw, minimum 45 mm (1¾ in), countersinking the heads into the board. Glue and screw blocks on the inside of the seat at the join in the chipboard between seat and back sides.

114

Diagram 61
Large unit chair and seat back with
arms detached

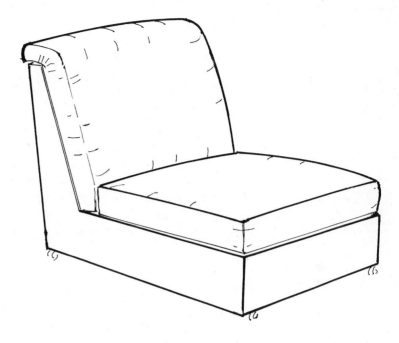

Diagram 62
Sectional view showing the
upholstery details

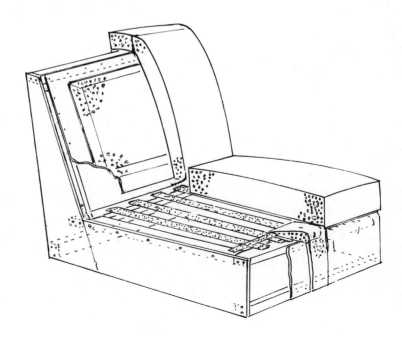

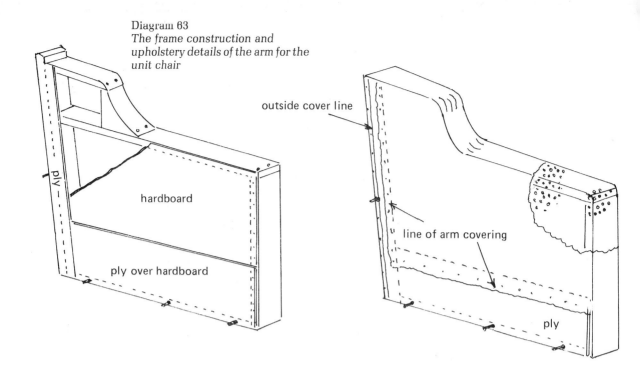

Diagram 63
The frame construction and upholstery details of the arm for the unit chair

outside cover line

ply

hardboard

ply over hardboard

line of arm covering

ply

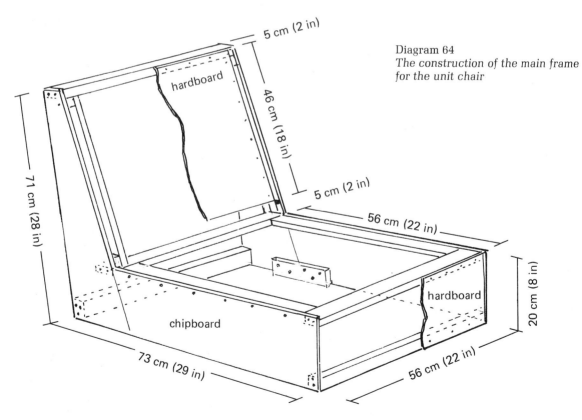

Diagram 64
The construction of the main frame for the unit chair

5 cm (2 in)

hardboard

46 cm (18 in)

5 cm (2 in)

56 cm (22 in)

71 cm (28 in)

20 cm (8 in)

hardboard

chipboard

73 cm (29 in)

56 cm (22 in)

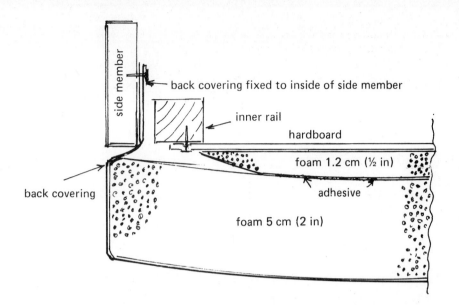

Diagram 65
Finishing the side of the chair back, showing the covering pushed through a gap in the frame

With the main body of the unit together, the upper side seat rails can be glued and screwed flush with the top edges of the side seat panels. The inner side back rails can also be fixed in position with spacing blocks at top and bottom; the blocks should give a clearance of 18 mm (¾ in) to allow the covering to be passed through. The hardboard back panel should be nailed to the inner side rails leaving the gap between the rails and the side panels, nailed also to the top back rail. The bottom edge of the hardboard should be left about 36 mm (1½ in) short of the seat rails. It is unnecessary to have this fixed and this space will allow the back covering to pass through. Cut the front border hardboard fit with edges flush with those of the frame.

Upholstery materials

Pirelli standard laminated rubber webbing 5 cm (2 in) wide, 3.6 m (12 ft)

Polyether or latex foam, firm density, 10 cm (4 in) thick, for seat cushion

Polyether or latex foam 5 cm (2 in) thick for inside back

Polyether or latex foam 5 cm (2 in) thick for seat lip

Polyether foam 12 mm (½ in) thick for centre inside back

Polyether foam 12 mm (½ in) thick for lining side panels, front border and outside back.

Covering 2.52 m of 122 cm width (2¾ yd of 4 ft width)

Foaming up and covering

Side panels　It is important to tailor the foam neatly and accurately with edges cut straight and square. The seat and back side panels should be lined with the 12 mm (½ in) foam, taking the foam over to the inner edge of the side upper seat rail and level with the base. The

117

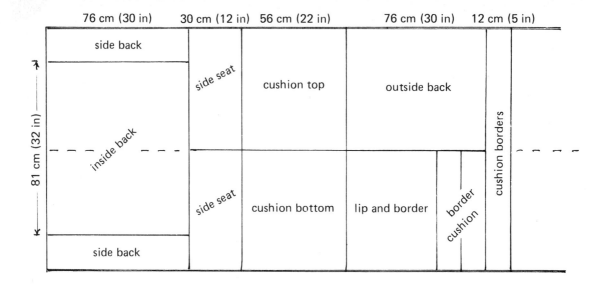

Diagram 66
Cover cutting plan for the seat and back of the unit chair, requiring a total amount of 2.5 m (2¾ yd) of fabric 127 cm (50 in) wide

side back panel should be lined to the back edge with the foam being tucked into the gap between the side facing and the inner rail. For reasons of economy the foam may be joined by butting edges together in the same places where the chipboard was joined. A few staples or small tacks spaced widely and close to the edges will hold it in position.

These panels can now be covered, again joining seat and back side panels for economy. The join may be machined or folded butted together and slip-stitched: if done well, a join such as this will not usually be noticed. Temporarily fixing the covering in the first instance will make it easier to line up the weave of the fabric with the base line of the seat, with the weave in the vertical direction at right angles to the base.

The covering should be fixed on the inner face edge of the seat rails and taken through the gap of the back and fixed on the inside of the side panel; the front edge of the covering should be taken round the corner and fixed on the face.

The seat   Five strands of 5 cm (2 in) webbing should be tacked or stapled front to back of the seat. With the back hardboard in position it is necessary to fix the webbing first on the seat back cross member and tension towards the front at approximately 10 per cent, fixing the webbing on the front seat rail.

A wedge shaped piece of foam cut from a 5 cm (2 in) piece should be prepared for the seat lip so that its thinner edge extends approximately 12.5 cm (5 in) from the front edge.

To provide a line for the lip and front border covering a length of rubber webbing should be tensioned across the seat so that its back edge is 12.5 cm (5 in) from the front of the seat. The front covering should be taken under this webbing, stapled on the top surface of the front rail with the wedge shaped piece of foam set in position, the front covering is brought over the foam from the back edge of the

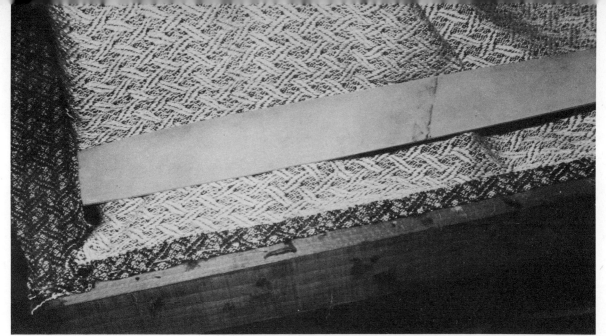

57 Rubber webbing tensioned across the seat to form the back line of the seat lip

58 The seat lip with the covering in position

webbing and down the front border which should have a lining of 12 mm (½ in) foam over the hardboard, fixing the covering on the underside of the bottom cross member the ends being pinned into position and finally slip-stitched to the side panel covering.

The back   To give a slight domed effect to the inside back a piece of 12 mm (½ in) foam should be cut approximately 5 cm (2 in) smaller all round than the hardboard nailed to the inside of the back. Chamfer all round this foam so that it has a feather edge then stick it in the centre of the hardboard. This should be done before the thicker back foam is cut; the underlay piece will affect the width of the main foam.

The 5 cm (2 in) main layer of foam for the back should be given the radius at the top of the back by cutting the edge at an angle and sticking a narrow strip along so that an inverted 'L' shape is formed; this will set better than a single piece bent over the top of the back.

The width of the foam should be fractionally greater than the width of the frame. Stick it along the top edge leaving the end 5 cm (2 in) free on both sides; the foam should not be stuck over the slots down each side. The bottom line of the foam can also be left unstuck.

The covering may now be laid over the back and attached with temporary tacking top and bottom, the top back to the outer edge of the top rail without reducing too much the depth of foam and the bottom line of covering to the seat cross member below the back hardboard. The sides of the covering should be tucked under the foam sides and pulled through the gaps at each side (diagram 65). The covering should be tensioned quite lightly, just enough to remove any slackness or fullness.

At the top corners of the back, beyond the position where the covering is able to go through the gap, the covering should be gathered up by threading twine in and out of the covering using a small circular needle in a position which will enable the covering to tuck under the foam (which has been left unstuck), by tacking one end of the twine through the gap, then pulling the other end and easing the covering into small pleats around the radius, tacking the twine on the outside top back. With the covering set correctly it may be finally tacked or stapled home.

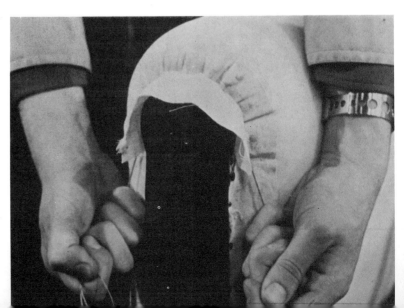

59 Gathering small pleats by means of twine threaded through the material and pulled tight

Fluted covering easy chair with adjustable arms. Tweed covering. Designed by Mike Jesky. L.C.F.

Chair with chromed steel under-
framing. Acrylic velvet covering.
Designed by Kenneth Holden. L.C.F.

Covering for the outside back should be back-tacked, along the upper edge of the top back rail, taken under the bottom cross member, folded under down the side edges, pinned temporarily and then slip-stitched.

The seat cushion   It is now possible to cut the foam for the seat cushion accurately, again cutting fractionally oversize to give tension to the outer covering. Use a template made from stout paper or card when cutting to ensure acuracy of fit when the covering is machined. If arms are to be fitted the cushion should not overlap the sides of the seat.

Covering the webbing

Diagram 67 shows a method of forming a platform or apron to enclose individual strands of webbing which may be employed for this seating unit. A good quality lining or plain fabric should be used, two thicknesses of the lining being used with lines machined to form pockets running from back to front for the webbing to be threaded through. The two side edges of the lining are hemmed and strands of elastic are sewn to the hemmed back edge, elastic being tacked to the same seat back member as the webbing.

The webbing should be tacked on first and threaded through the channels before being tensioned and tacked or stapled to the front member. The front of the lining platform is then tacked down and the cross web forming the lip stretched across over.

Diagram 67
Encasing the rubber seat webbing with a linen apron to give a neater appearance and to preserve the webbing

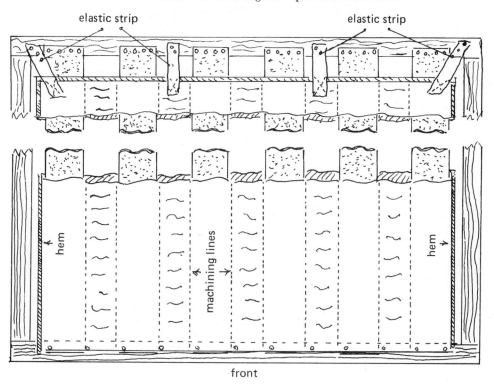

elastic strip   elastic strip

hem   machining lines   hem

front

121

Constructing the arm section

An arm suitable for attaching to the unit is shown in diagram 63 with construction details. The method of attaching the arm to the main unit is with 10 cm (4 in) 6 mm (¼ in) diameter bolts protruding from the inner base member with one approximately half way up the back member—all to line up with holes drilled in the unit. The height and depth of the arm is identical to the height and depth of the unit so that the top and front of the arm line up with the unit when all are upholstered.

The width of the timber (preferably beech) is 62 mm (2½ in). Both sides of the arm are lined with hardboard or plywood nailed in position flush with all edges. In addition an extra layer of hardboard of the same thickness should be nailed along one side at the base (the width to coincide with the chipboard side of the unit) plus a narrow strip nailed vertically at the back. This treatment will make this the inside of the arm. If a pair of arms are being made the additional strips should be on the reverse side of the other arm. The recess formed by these additional pieces will, provided the foam is cut away along the lines of the inner edges, allow the arm to bolt up tight and rigid to the unit without compressing the foam.

Holes to house the bolts should be drilled and the bolts inserted before the hardboard is nailed on the outside of the arm so that with domed headed bolts countersunk flush with the face of the timber the hardboard will prevent the bolt from being pushed out when the bolting up is being done. The nuts may be screwed on the bolts, after the upholstery of the unit, from the inside of the seat side member. The bolt half way up the back can have the nut put on while the outside back is left free temporarily until the bolting has been accomplished.

Upholstering the arm unit

The inside and outside of the arms should be lined first with 12 mm (½ in) foam, cutting the inside piece short in line with the rebate provided by the extra hardboard. The top and front edges should have thicker foam, i.e. 2.5 cm (1 in). Due to the shape of the arm it is impossible to wrap the covering around in one piece so a border is required which can be one piece from the front bottom edge to the top back.

The covering should be tailored carefully, allowing for seaming and using a plain seam only when machining. Ensure that the flanges of the seams do not become twisted while you are easing the covering into position. They should lay flat against the side panels and not under the border. The outside arm covering should be tacked or stapled on the underside of the arm along its bottom line, the back vertical line being taken around to the inside and fixed so that it will be hidden when bolted. The bottom and back lines of the inside arm should be fixed on to the extra pieces of hardboard, folded under at tacking lines for neatness. Once the arms are bolted in position, a bottoming fabric should be tacked on and the project finished off by fitting a set of castors or glides.

122

Easy Chair

The frame

The framework for this chair is made from straight lengths of timber without any shaping whatever and with very few construction problems for the woodworker or framemaker. Alternative methods of construction for the frame are also shown.

It has a wide solid front rail to the seat and the hardboard or plywood lining the inside arms is extended down to the side bottom member. This method of lining the inside arms allows the arm upholstery to be extended and finished on this lower rail on its inner face, so if resilient rubber webbing is used back to front without any covering over, the base of the arm is neat and tidy. Serpentine springing may also be used with insulation over, finishing the sides of the seat at the same fixing points as the arm covering.

The second method is shown in diagram 70. This allows the covering at the bottom of the arm to be taken through the space between the arm stay member and the side base member to be fixed on the outer face of the stay rail. Also, strands of rubber webbing can be applied from side to side.

Should serpentine springing be used instead of rubber webbing, an additional member would be needed across the back between the back legs, at the same height as the front upper seat member.

Upholstery materials

Foam
Arms (2) 46 by 12.5 cm by 2.5 cm (1 ft 6 in by 5 in by 1 in), firm density
Arms (2) 46 by 61 by 1.2 cm (1 ft 6 in by 2 ft by ½ in), medium density
Wing pieces (2) 30 by 30 by 2.5 cm (1 ft by 1 ft by 1 in), medium density
Back 76 by 61 by 5 cm (2 ft 6 in by 2 ft by 2 in), medium density
Back 46 by 38 by 2.5 cm (1 ft 6 in by 1 ft 3 in by 1 in), medium density
Lip 12.5 by 53 by 2.5 cm (5 in by 1 ft 9 in by 1 in), firm density
Border 15 by 53 by 1.2 cm (6 in by 1 ft 9 in by ½ in), medium density
Cushion 53.5 by 53.5 by 10 cm (1 ft 9 in by 1 ft 9 in by 4 in), firm density
Standard 5 cm (2 in) rubber webbing, 6 m (6½ yd) (seat and back)
Bottoming 61 by 61 cm (2 ft by 2 ft)
Covering 3.2 m (3½ yd)

Diagram 68
Small easy chair with simple upholstery

Diagram 69
Construction of small easy chair, with a wide front rail and plywood lining inside the arms and wings, suitable for rubber webbing or serpentine spring suspension

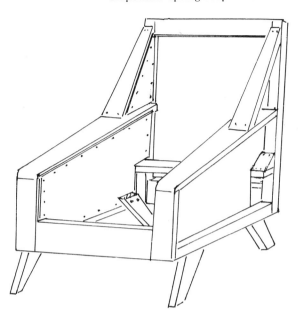

Diagram 70
Alternative method of frame construction suitable for webbing the seat from side to side, with the arms finishing above the seat webbing

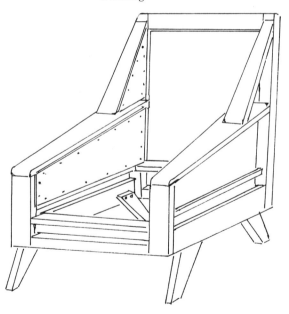

Diagram 71
*Sectional view of the upholstery
details of the chair*

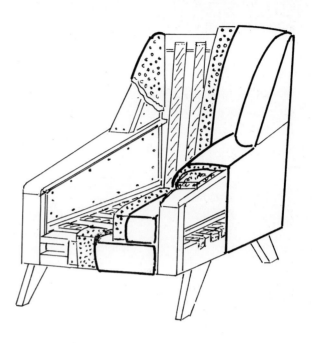

Diagram 72
*Cover cutting plan for the small easy
chair, requiring a total amount of
3.2 m (3½ yd) of fabric 127 cm (50 in)
wide*

51 cm (20 in)	36 cm (14 in)	89 cm (35 in)	selvedge 58 cm (23 in)	46 cm (18 in)	26 cm (5 in) (10 in) 12 cm

join*				join* *	
inside arm	outside arm	outside back	cushion bottom	outside wing	seat lip
				inside wing	
half width					half width
inside arm	outside arm	inside back	cushion top	inside wing	cushion border
				outside wing	
join*				join*	

127 cm (50 in)

selvedge

The arm

Upholstery of the arms consists of an underlay of 25 mm (1 in) firm density foam along the arm top, this being stuck in position. Covering this is a piece of 1.2 cm (½ in) foam from the bottom of the inside arm over the foam on the top of the arm and ending flush with the outside line; this is stuck in position with only a line of adhesive approximately 5 cm (2 in) wide around the edges to conserve adhesive. Foam for the arm front should be carried around from the inside of the arm, trimming surplus foam away at the corner and butting the edges together neatly.

The filling for the wing is a piece of 25 mm (1 in) foam over the hardboard and over the face member. The wing should be upholstered after the arm has been covered.

The back

Suspension for the back can be five strands resilient rubber webbing (or indeed serpentine springing) for either method of frame construction. Filling for the back should be a medium density 5 cm (2 in) thickness of foam; to achieve a domed effect an additional piece of 25 mm (1 in) foam may be laid under the central area of the back. To hold the foam in position a strip of calico should be stuck along the top and bottom and then fixed to the frame.

The lip and covering

The inside and outside arm coverings are tailored and machined together so that the seam runs along the outside top and front edges. The front lip is upholstered as shown in plates 57-58. If the frame is constructed as in diagram 69 a piece of hardboard or plywood should be cut to the width between the arms and to a depth of approximately 12.5 cm (5 in). Nail this to the seat front edge with the covering under, put the foam on top of the board then bring the covering over and tack it under the front rail.

Cut the inside back covering to size, lay it over the foam with a light tension and tack or staple it home. The outside wings should be temporarily pinned along the sloping front edge and tacked around the back and under the outside arm before this is finished off. The outside back covering may be back-tacked along the outside upper edge, fixed to the underside of the base rail, temporarily pinned along the side edges and finally slip-stitched at the same time as the outside wings.

A bottom covering of black linen or hessian should cover the base if the covering on the underside has not been turned under.

The cushion foam should be cut to size and a covering tailored to fit snugly with a slight tension.

Deep-sprung Armchair

This is a luxuriously upholstered chair with pleasing sculptured curves designed to fit into a modern decor. Having more shaping and a more difficult and a complicated method of upholstery than the previous types, this requires rather more skill to make than the examples described previously.

The Frame

The frame for this chair has an amount of shaping to some of its members with double back and side stay rails which are necessary for the method of upholstery employed for this style. Seat suspension is by the use of a spring unit. By fitting a wide front seat member, this supports the unit right up to the front giving the added comfort of a deep sprung edge to the seat.

The framework of a chair of this nature must be well constructed with sound timber and cramped up tightly dowelled joints. Construction of the frame involves making up the two complete arm and wing sections as separate units (paired), then cramping them together with the cross members. Note that the top arm members are set 18 mm (¾ in) lower than the top edge of the heads (face pieces).

Drilling of 10 mm (⅜ in) dowel holes in all members should be undertaken before assembly; it is most important that the holes are drilled squarely and in line with their opposite numbers to prevent any splitting of timber while the joints are being cramped. One, two or three dowels are used depending upon the size of timber being joined. The complete frame should be assembled and roughly cleaned before it is upholstered.

Diagram 73
A deep sprung, fully upholstered chair

Diagram 74
Frame construction for the fully upholstered chair

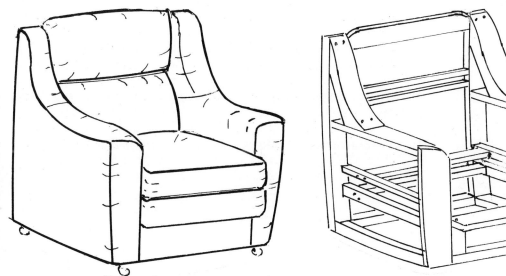

Upholstery Materials

Seat spring unit

Serpentine springing (11 SWG) 4 m (13 ft)

Webbing (jute or linen) 2 m (6 ft 6 in)

Hessian, medium quality, 1.5 m (5 ft)

Coir fibre padding: back 61 cm by 1 m (2 by 3 ft); seat 61 by 61 cm (2 ft by 2 ft)

Foam

Inside arms (2) 12.5 by 38 by 2.5 cm (5 in by 1 ft 3 in by 1 in), firm density

Inside arms (2) 50 by 76 by 1.2 cm (1 ft 8 in by 2 ft 6 in by ½ in), medium density

Outside arms (2) 90 by 50 by 1.2 cm (3 ft by 1 ft 8 in by ½ in), medium density

Inside top arms (2) 41 by 50 by 2.5 cm (1 ft 4 in by 1 ft 8 in by 1 in), medium density

Outside top arms (2) 30 by 30 by 1.2 cm (1 ft by 1 ft by ½ in), medium density

Top back 46 by 61 by 3.6 cm (1 ft 6 in by 2 ft by 1½ in), soft density

Bottom back 61 by 61 by 3.6 cm (2 ft by 2 ft by 1½ in), medium density

Seat platform lip 56 by 76 by 1.2 cm (1 ft 10 in by 2 ft 6 in by ½ in), medium density

Bottom border 15 by 60 by 1.2 cm (6 in by 2 ft by ½ in), medium density

Platform lining 76 by 76 cm (2 ft 6 in by 2 ft 6 in)

Bottoming 68 by 68 cm (2 ft 3 in by 2 ft 3 in)

Covering 4.5 m (5 yd)

The arms

Upholstery of the two arms and wing pieces should be undertaken first. Three strands of webbing (jute or linen) should be tacked or stapled, evenly spaced, along the inner edge of the upper of the two stay members (using 10 mm (⅜ in) tacks if tacks are being used), taking care not to damage the joints and hand straining the webbing only. Fix the webbing to the inner face of the top arm member.

Line the inside arm tightly with a medium quality hessian, fixing on the same horizontal rails as the web, also to the vertical face member and the back leg on the inside edges. The outside arm should also be lined with a similar hessian but leaving the lower half free to be fixed later.

Two pieces of firm density foam should be cut to fit the top arm member flush with the side edges, up to the raised front face and to the leading edge of the wing piece and stuck in position. 25 mm (1 in) foam, medium density, covers the inside arm from the top inner stay rail, carrying over the top of the underlay piece to the outside edge

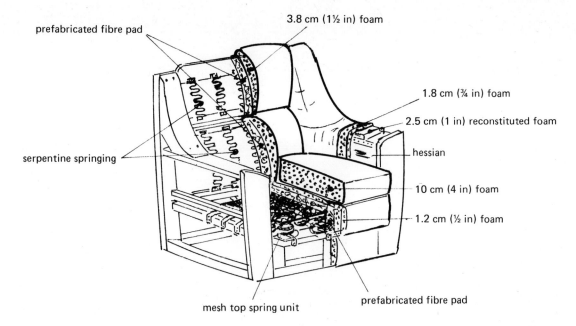

prefabricated fibre pad

3.8 cm (1½ in) foam

1.8 cm (¾ in) foam

2.5 cm (1 in) reconstituted foam

hessian

serpentine springing

10 cm (4 in) foam

1.2 cm (½ in) foam

mesh top spring unit

prefabricated fibre pad

Diagram 75
A sectional view of the upholstery of the deep sprung chair

flush with the front and approximately 5 cm (2 in) short of the back leg. Only the edges of this need be stuck.

12 mm (½ in) foam should be laid on and tailored to cover the outside arm, from the outside top arm to the base of the frame and from the back leg forward to the inside line of the front face. Trim it neatly and stick accurately, leaving the lower outside arm free as with the hessian. A 25 cm (1 in) piece of foam should be stuck over the wing pieces and trimmed carefully to make a curve which will butt up tightly with the arm to give a continuous surface.

It is more convenient to cover the arms and wing shapes before proceeding with any further upholstery. The covering should be cut as shown in the cover cutting plan. Check the measurements first.

Three pieces of covering are needed for each arm, i.e. inside and outside arms and wing pieces. These pieces should be laid on the foam, trimmed to shape and pinned together with the reverse side out to avoid having to unpin and turn the covering before machining.

The outside arms and the wings are cut all in one piece unlike the insides which are in two separate pieces; diagram 75 shows the position of the join of the inside arm and wing piece. The seam of arm, which should be piped, runs along the top outer edge, across the top face and down the inside facing. Piping is allowed for in the cutting plan. After easing the covering into position, the bottom half of the outside arm should be temporarily left free.

Inside backs

The serpentine springing method makes an ideal base for this type of back upholstered in two sections. Five strands of 11 SWG should be fixed vertically on each back with a basic insulation of coir fibre prefabricated padding over. 3.6 cm (1½ in) soft density foam is needed for the upper section of the back with a firmer density if

129

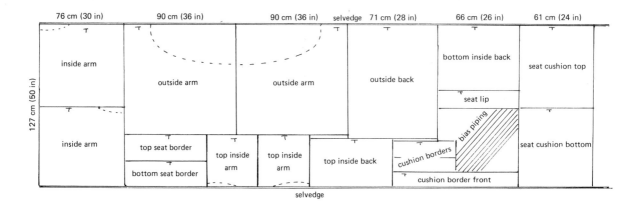

Diagram 76
Cover cutting plan for the fully upholstered chair, requiring a total amount of 4.6 m (5 yd) of fabric 127cm (50 in) wide.
N.B. Covering in this instance is planned 'on the run' with plain fabric, i.e. using warp yarn across the width of upholstery

possible for the lower section. The top and bottom edges of these pieces should have flanges of calico or linen stuck along them so they may be used for fixing the foam in position.

The covering pieces for the two sections of the back are rectangular, the lower section taking rather more up and down. To economise on the width of covering, hessian flys may be sewn down the side edges; when the covering is set in position the flys are fixed on the inner surface of the back legs. At the break between the two backs the covering of both backs is taken through the opening between the two cross members and fixed on the back surfaces.

The seat

The illustration shows a spring unit providing deep springing without the traditional method of hand springing being used. A unit of the correct size should, of course, be used, i.e. having a clearance of approximately 18 mm (¾ in) between the side stay members and the same clearance short of the back cross member. The unit should have 16 springs, 15 cm (6 in) height 10 SWG, steel lath fixing as shown in diagram 8.

Insulation immediately over the mesh top of the spring unit should be prefabricated coir fibre padding with 12 mm (½ in) foam over or rubberised hair (if rubberised hair, a covering of hessian should be used over the unit). Fixing for the fibre padding should be on to the lower stay rails (back and side) and to the front edge of the projecting front member.

Covering of the seat should be part lining with a lip of covering at the front for 12.5 cm (5 in) back from the front edge, the lining and the covering being machined together, the flange of the seam being used to sew twine through to give a slight indentation to ensure a completely flat seat to carry a cushion. Immediately under the platform (back section of seat) and the lip should be 12 mm (½ in) foam. The lip foam extending to the bottom border, the front lip covering is piped on the edge.

A lower seat border should be back-tacked immediately below the projecting spring edge seat rail; the lip and top border covering should be covering the underside of the projection.

Diagram 77
*Sinking the join between the lip
covering and the platform lining; the
flange of the join between the lip
covering and the platform lining
is sewn through the seat filling with
a long needle and twine*

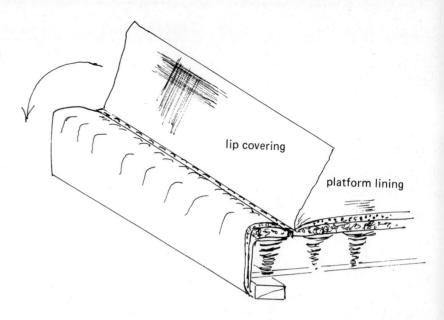

lip covering

platform lining

To finish off the upholstery of the chair, the outside back may be back-tacked along the outer top edges to reinforce the covering. Hessian should be tacked or stapled across first, then the covering laid over, fixed to the underside of the base frame, temporarily pinned down the side edges and finally slip-stitched. To complete, a neat bottoming of black linen or hessian should be tacked or stapled over the raw edges of the covering.

The cushion interior foam should be a medium density good quality 10 cm (4 in) thick foam cut fractionally oversize. Care should be taken in cutting the covering so that when piped it is not too tight a fit causing wrinkling. If a domed cushion is required two 5 cm (2 in) pieces of foam should be faced together with a 12 mm (½ in) smaller piece sandwiched between.

131

Period Wing Chair

An ever-popular style of upholstered chair, modern productions of this type of chair have utilised a number of modern upholstery methods and materials and so considerably reduced the high degree of craftmanship necessary to upholster the originals of this style and, in so doing, have also reduced the amount of time which would have been involved.

Diagram 78 shows a cut-through section of a typical wing chair currently produced, utilising tension springing for seat and back suspension. Pirelli resilient rubber webbing would adequately replace the tension springing in this instance. Diagram 79 gives a cover cutting plan.

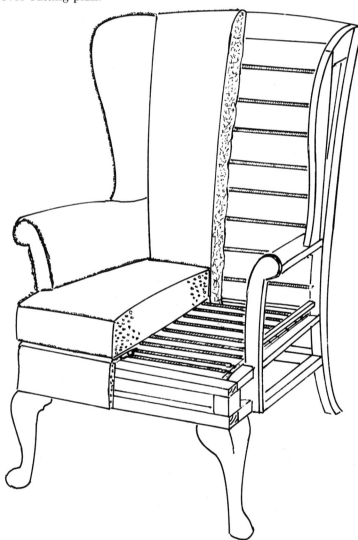

Diagram 78
A wing easy chair showing a sectional view

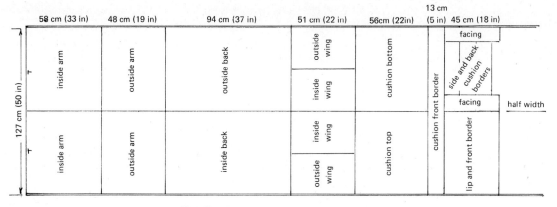

The diagram shows column widths across the top: 58 cm (33 in), 48 cm (19 in), 94 cm (37 in), 51 cm (22 in), 56cm (22in), 13 cm (5 in), 45 cm (18 in). The left side shows 127 cm (50 in). Labels within the cutting plan include: inside arm, outside arm, outside back, outside wing, inside wing, cushion bottom, facing, side and back cushion borders, cushion front border, facing, half width, inside arm, outside arm, inside back, inside wing, outside wing, cushion top, lip and front border.

Diagram 79
Cover cutting plan for the wing easy chair, requiring a total amount of 3.7 m (4 yd) of fabric 1.4 m (54 in) wide

The frame

The framework for this chair is fairly light with a number of shaped members, cabriole shaped front legs and curved back legs. The amateur woodworker is unlikely to have the facilities or the ability to make this frame and it is probably best left to the professional frame-maker.

Upholstery Materials

Tension springs (plastic covered or braided for seat);
seat, 9 springs 14 SWG 41 cm (1 ft 4 in) long, 2 fixing plates;
back, 6 springs 18 SWG plus 2 springs 14 SWG, lengths as seat uncovered.
Jute or linen webbing 1.4 m (4 ft 6 in)
Hessian, medium quality 1.2 m (4 ft)
Foam
Arms (2) 56 by 50 by 3.6 cm (1 ft 10 in by 1 ft 8 in by 1½ in), firm density
Facings (2) 50 by 12.5 by 1.2 cm (1 ft 8 in by 5 in by ½ in), medium density
Back 76 by 60 by 5 cm (2 ft 6 in by 2 ft by 2 in), medium density
Lip 60 by 12.5 by 3.6 cm (2 ft by 5 in by 1½ in), firm density
Border 86 by 15 by 1.2 cm (2 ft 10 in by 6 in by ½ in), medium density
Wings (2) 46 by 30 by 2.5 cm (1 ft 6 in by 1 ft by 1 in), medium density
Cushion 56 by 56 by 10 cm (1 ft 10in by 1 ft 10 in by 4 in), firm density
Covering
Ruche 4 m (13 ft)
Bottoming 61 by 61 cm (2 by 2 ft)

The arms

Upholstery of the inside arms should be undertaken first. Two strands of webbing (jute or linen) should be applied on the inner faces of the arm stay rail and top arm rail covered with a medium

133

quality hessian; an amount of surplus hessian should be allowed along the top edge so that it may form a pad when taken over the top arm rail and filled with evenly placed off-cuts of foam. The pad should fill the small step down from the front of the arm to the arm rail, tapering gently to the back of the arm leaving the base of the wing clear of filling.

Foam 36 mm (1½ in) should be laid over the hessian and pad and fixed in position with strips of calico stuck along its top and bottom edges and tacked or stapled to the outside of the bottom arm stay rail and under the top arm rail. 12 mm (½ in) pieces of foam should be trimmed to the shape of the facing scroll and stuck neatly to the edge of the arm foam; the facing foam should extend to the extreme bottom of the facing.

The covering of the arm should be ruched on the front edge and machined only to the underside of the radius of the scroll, the remainder being left free to be tacked or stapled along the side of the facing after the covering has been fixed home.

Inside back

This should be upholstered after the arms. A covering of medium quality hessian should be tacked or stapled over the tension springs. It is important that this hessian is left with an amount of fullness or slackness by pleating. 5 cm (2 in) medium density foam, cut to fit between arms and wings, is fixed in position as with the arms, with strips of calico top and bottom and fixed to the outside top back and the bottom back stay. The back covering has no machining; a rectangular piece of covering, laid over the foam and lightly eased, cuts around the stiles.

Wing pieces

(These should be upholstered after the back). The covering for the inside wing should be back-tacked at its base where it meets the arm as a first operation, a piece of linen/jute webbing should then be tacked with a piece of hessian over the back-tacked covering. The webbing should be hand strained up to the top of the wing with its back edge tight against the surface of the back, afterwards bringing the hessian tightly up to give a firm platform for the filling, the back line of the hessian should be folded in line with the back edge of the webbing.

A 2.5 cm (1 in) layer of foam cut to shape will suffice for the filling and may be held in position by the covering only, without any need for fixing strips. It will be necessary to snip the covering along the curve of the bottom of the wing.

Seat lip and border

The first step towards upholstery is to screw two tension spring holding plates, one each side of the seat on the inner edge of the upper seat rails. The tension springs can then be hooked in place, fixed at a tension of 8.5 per cent, i.e. 2.5 to 30 cm (1 in to 1 ft) before you start work on the seat lip.

The covering of the seat lip and border should be tacked reverse side on to the top seat rail, taken under the second tension spring and back over the foam on the front edge and border to be tacked under the base front member. The gap between the two front rails should be lined either with hessian or ply, with 12 mm (½ in) foam over and a 36 mm (1½ in) wedge shaped piece on the top edge.

Outside arms and back

The top edge of the outside arm covering should be back-tacked under the arm rail below the scroll, lined with hessian for reinforcement and the front edge slip-stitched along the ruche line down the side of the facing, the back edge being fixed at the back of the back leg. The outside back should be slip-stitched around top and side edges first lined with hessian; should the top of the back have a straight edge, this may be back-tacked.

135

A neat bottom cover should be the final touch to the upholstery.

The seat cushion

A good quality medium density foam of 10 cm (4 in) thickness should be used for the cushion. If possible, a moulded domed latex cushion should be obtained. Diagram 78 shows a wing chair with short 'ear' pieces on the front edges of the cushion but, rather than cut this shape from a large piece of foam, you can stick the ear pieces on as long as you make sure the width and length are accurately measured. The cushion should be ruched all around both edges, leaving a back edge and a short distance up the sides open for inserting the interior.

An added refinement to the cushion to ensure that the ruched line around the top keeps its position, is to machine a flange of calico to the seaming along the top front edge and, before fitting the covering, to stick the flange to the front edge of the foam in its correct position. The cushion case should be left open approximately half way along the sides of the bottom panel so the foam may be folded to draw the covering on more easily.

Fixed-cushion Chair

This simple example of an upholstered chair utilises three fixed cushions. Details of the frame and upholstery of this chair are shown in diagram 80 together with suggested sizes; these may be varied as desired.

The upholstery of the frame is minimal, the covering of the sides, front and outside back being tacked or stapled to the frame. The seat and two back cushions are filled with foam tailored to the desired shape and sizes. Covering for the cushions is made up with flanges sewn in appropriate positions to pass through the opening between the front seat rails and fix on the upper centre back member.

The back seat cushion and bottom back are fixed with flanges tacked to the seat stay rail.

Diagram 80
A modern easy chair with three fixed seat and back cushions, showing the frame and upholstery details

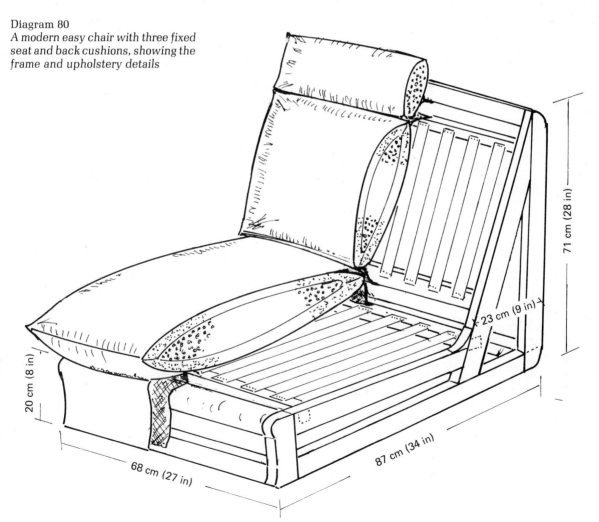

87 cm (34 in)

68 cm (27 in)

20 cm (8 in)

23 cm (9 in)

71 cm (28 in)

Glossary

Back-tacking   Method of attaching covering to conceal tacking on outside backs and arms with straight edges.

Bias cutting   Cutting fabric diagonally across threads.

Bible front   A bold rounded edge to front of seat.

Blind stitch   Stitches formed with twine to consolidate filling.

Bottoming   A muslin or hessian cover tacked to the underside of upholstery.
also: the sitter flattening the filling of a cushion chair to the base.

Bridle ties   Loops of twine to hold filling in place.

Burlap   see Hessian.

Buttoning   Method of forming deep diamond shapes with carefully positioned buttons.

Calico   White muslin (fine cotton) material, available in a variety of weights, used for undercovering or bottoming.

Cavity foam   Foam made with openings on one side. The weight and resiliency is determined by thickness, and by diameter of cavities. For reversible cushions, two pieces are glued together with cavities facing.

Chamfer   An edge that is shaved or rounded, required when making a bevel on a corner of timber, or joining two welts of leather.

Chipboard   Fabricated timber board manufactured from compressed wood chips.

Coil springs   Steel wire spirals, available in various sizes and wire gauges.

Collar   Strip of material fitted round shaped cuts (e.g. show-wood arms) to prevent gaping when stiles are cut.

Cotton felt   Cotton lap used to cover loose fillings to create a smooth surface. Available in rolls or by the yard; thickness is determined by weight per yard/metre.

D.I.Y.   Abbreviation for do-it-yourself.

Deck (see Platform)   Area under a removable cushion on a sprung seat. A sturdy coordinating fabric is machined to top covering just past the well to cover this concealed area.

Doming   Degree of rise in centre of seat or cushion.

Double cone spring   Spring with large top and bottom coil and narrow waist.

Dowels   Grooved wooden pegs glued into predrilled holes to form furniture frame joints.

Drop-in seat   A loose seat to fit into rebate of dining chair or bedroom stool.

Dust cover   see Bottoming.

Fibre filling   Loose stuffing used to soften and shape the spring and frame edges.

Fillets   Additional small pieces of timber added to frame.

Flange   Strip of material for fixing purposes.

Float buttoning   Buttons lightly pulled into covering.

Fly   Extension piece of hessian, etc, machine stitched to final cover where it will not be seen, to economise with covering.

Fullness   Surplus covering causing wrinkling.

Gauge   Thickness of wire used to make spiral springs, the lowest number representing the thickest wire and the highest number the the finest.

Gimp   Narrow woven decorative tape used to cover tacks and raw edges on show-wood furniture; available in a variety of textures and colours.

Gimp pins   Fine tacks with small heads to hold gimp and cover in place; virtually invisible in use.

Glasspaper   Sandpaper used to smooth rough edges on furniture frames, and to clean excess glue from joints.

Gutter   A channel formed in hessian for spring edge.

Hessian   A rough woven jute cloth, also known as burlap.

Join   A machine-stitched seam used to connect two pieces of fabric.

K.D. (Knock down)   Furniture made in separate parts for ease of transport.

Laidcord   Heavy cord made from flax or hemp fibre for lashing springs. 'Laid' refers to the method of manufacture, which makes the cord stretch-resistant.

Lashing   The lacing and knotting together of spring coils with heavy twine to prevent lateral movement.

Laminated webbing   Rubber webbing with rayon threads within layers of rubber.

Latex   Foam manufactured from natural rubber.

Lead moulding   Trimming for leather upholstery to hide tacks or gimp pins.

Linterfelt   Thick padding of cotton fibres (see Cotton felt).

Lip   Front edge of cushion seat.

Loft   Bulkiness, resilience.

Mock cushion   Construction of seat to imitate a cushion.

Mortice, mortise   Hole cut into timber to accommodate a tenon (projection) to form a mortice and tenon joint.

Picking   Separating and fluffing up hard-packed portions of fibre stuffing by hand or machine.

Pin-stuffed   An upholstery seat using one layer of filling only.

Pincers   Pliers used to extract small tacks and staples from furniture frames.

Pincore   A latex foam with fine pinhole cavities.

Piping   See Welt.

Platform   Rear surface of cushion seat.

Plywood gusset   A triangular piece of plywood used to strengthen joints.

Pull-over edge   A seat front edge with covering 'pulled' straight over.

Rebate   A recess or groove cut near the edge of the frame to support a drop-in seat or to provide a tacking area.

Refurbishing   Repairing or renewing.

Ripping   Stripping of covering or filling from frame.

Roll edge   A roll edge prevents stuffing from working away from the edge of the frame. Commercially made rolls can be purchased by the yard.

Ruche   Decorative trimming to hide join in covering.

Sash cramp   A bar or pipe clamp used when regluing loose joints.

Scrim   Open or loosely woven fabric made from flax yarn.

Serpentine spring   Continuous wire spring formed from zigzag strip, requiring no webbing.

Show-wood chair   An upholstered frame with polished wood showing.

Silencer   Strip of webbing or sturdy material placed between the unfastened spring coils and frame to prevent rattling when the depressed springs hit the wood.

Single cone spring   Spring with large top coil with rest tapering to base.

Sinuous spring   see Serpentine spring.

Skewers   Long upholsterers' pins with ring at one end.

Skivering   Shaving the underside of leather to reduce thickness.

Spring edge   A flexible edge for seats or backs.

Squab   Flat firmly-stuffed cushion.

Stile   Part of frame construction around which covering must be cut.

Stitched edge   A padded edge formed over the front of the spring burlap to create the desired finished shape.

Stuffover chair   Chair completely stuffed over and covered.

SWG   Standard wire gauge.

Tack roll   Method of making a soft edge on a timber frame.

Tack ties   Lines caused in covering through faulty tacking.

Tacking strips   Narrow cardboard strips used to reinforce tacked final covering edges.

Tension spring   Elongated expanding spring for seats and backs.

Top stuffed   Interior upholstery applied to top surface of seat members only and not within the frame.

Trestles   Saw horses built with raised edges so that furniture will not slip off.

Under the edge   Forming an overlapping roll on the front of the seat.

Unit spring   An assembly of springs to fit a seat or back.

Vandyking   Method of joining covering for diamond buttoning.

Warp   Threads running down length of fabric, parallel to selvedge.

Webbing   Strips woven from jute, flax and cotton fibre to provide support for filling materials.

Weft   Threads running across width of fabric.

Well   A depression formed behind the first row of springs in a lashed spring seat.

Welt   A cord covered with diagonally cut strips of covering or contrasting fabric.

List of Addresses

Associations and Societies

Association of Master Upholsterers (AMU)
Dormar House, Mitre Ridge,
Scrubbs Lane, London NW10

British Furniture Manufacturers Federated Associations (BFM)
30 Harcourt Street,
London W1H 2AA

British Standards Institute (BSI)
2 Park Street, London W1A 2BS

City and Guilds of London Institute
76 Portland Place,
London W1N 4AA

The Design Centre
28 Haymarket, London SW1Y 4SU

Furniture Industry Research Association (FIRA)
Maxwell Road, Stevenage, Herts

Furniture and Timber Industry Training Board (FTITB)
31 Octagon Parade,
High Wycombe, Bucks

Furniture and Timber & Allied Trades Union (FTAT)
Fairfields, Roe Green, Kingsbury,
London NW9 0PT

London and South Eastern Furniture Manufacturers Association (LFM)
93 Great Eastern Street,
London EC2A 3JE

Scottish Furniture Manufacturers Association
Gordon Chambers,
90 Mitchell Street, Glasgow C1

Worshipful Company of Furniture Makers
c/o John Ward & Co,
Robertsbridge, Sussex

Society of Designer Craftsmen
6 Queen Square, London WC2

Colleges

The following colleges offer courses in furniture making including upholstery. Where demand exists some offer part-time classes.

St Albans: College of Building
Birmingham: Polytechnic
Brighton: Polytechnic
Bristol: Brunel Technical College
Bridgend: Technical College
Burnley: Technical College
Cambridge: College of Arts and Technology
Edinburgh: Telford College
Glasgow: College of Building & Printing
Huddersfield: Technical College
Hull: Technical College
High Wycombe: College of Art and Technology
Ipswich: Civic College
Kirkcaldy: Technical College
Leicester: Southfields College
Liverpool: College of Further Education
Leeds: Jacob Kramer
London: College of Furniture
Manchester: College of Building
Norwich: City College
Nottingham: Basford Hall
Newcastle: College of Arts and Technology
Portsmouth: Highbury College
Sheffield: Shirecliffe College
Southend: College of Technology
Sunderland: Wearsdale College of Further Education
Tottenham: Technical College
West Bromwich: College of Technology
Wisbech: Isle of Ely College of Further Education

Suppliers

UK

Wholesale suppliers for the professional and educational markets (mail and National Carrier delivery service)

C.K. Supplies
Ground Floor, Stubbs Mill,
1 Percy Street,
Ancoats, Manchester 4

M. Donaldson Ltd
4/8 Temperance Street,
Torquay, Devon TQ2 5PX

Dunlop Semtex Ltd
Industrial Products Division,
Chester Road, Erdington,
Birmingham B35 7AL

Dunlopillo Industrial Division
Cressex Industrial Estate,
Coronation Road,
High Wycombe, Bucks

D.L. Forster
17 Tramway Avenue, Stratford,
London E15 4PG

A.C. Freeman & Sons Ltd
Cromwell Road, Boscombe,
Bournemouth, Hants BH5 2JW

Glover Brothers
5 Redchurch Street, Shoreditch,
London E2

Jacksons (Upholsterers Supplies Ltd)
368 Argyle Street, Glasgow C2

James John & Sons
Studley, Warwickshire

Pirelli Ltd, GRG Division,
Derby Road, Burton-on-Trent,
Staffs

Porter Nicholson
Portland House, Norlington Road,
Leyton, London E10

Senco Pneumatics (UK) Ltd
Turner Road, Abbotsinch Estate,
Paisley PA3 4ER

J. Singleton Ltd
Red Bank, North Street,
Manchester M8 8QF

Retail outlets for the amateur market

D.L. Forster
17 Tramway Avenue, Stratford,
London E15 4PG

Upon receipt of enquiry this establishment will forward details of local distributors of upholstery sundries for the amateur: basic tools, tacks, cut lengths of hessian, calico, lining, rubber webbing and clips, Dacron filling, foam, etc.

Foam for Comfort
Dept SK
25 Tinshill Lane, Leeds LS16 6BU

Home Upholstery Supplies
14 Anne Road
Wellingborough, Northants

USA

Some of the firms listed below may sell only wholesale or in bulk quantities. Request the name of a distributor in your area. For an alternative source, contact a local upholsterer who can probably sell you what you need.

Fabric
Crompton-Richmond Co., Inc.
1071 Avenue of the Americas,
New York, N.Y. 10018

Ford Motor Co.
Chemical Products Div.,
3001 T Miller Rd.,
Dearborn, Mich. 48120

F. Schumacher & Co.
939 Third Ave, New York, N.Y. 10022

J.P. Stevens & Co.
1185 Avenue of the Americas,
New York, N.Y. 10036

Fiber
Blocksom & Co.
406 Center St., Michigan City,
Ind. 46360

Duracote Corp.
358 N. Diamond St.,
Ravenna, Ohio 44266

Excelsior, Inc.
726 Chestnut St., Rockford, Ill. 61102

International Textile, Inc.
2610 N. Pulaski Rd.,
Chicago, Ill. 60639

Universal Fibres, Inc.
65 9 St., Brooklyn, N.Y. 11215

Foam
Accurate Foam Co.
819 Fox St., La Porte, Ind. 46350

Fairmont Corp.
625 N. Michigan Ave., Chicago,
Ill. 60611

Firestone Foam Products Co.
823 Waterman Ave, P.O. Box 4159,
E. Providence, R.I. 02914

Foamage, Inc.
506 S. Garland, Orlando, Fla. 32801

Perma Foam, Inc.
605-R 21 St., Irvington, N.J. 07111

Springs
Barber Mfg. Co., Inc.
1824 Brown St., P.O. Box 2454,
Anderson, Ind. 46016

Dudek & Bock Spring Mfg. Co.
5102 W. Roosevelt Rd., Chicago,
Ill. 60650

Select-A-Spring Corp.
190 Railroad Ave, Jersey City,
N.J. 07302

Starcraft Mfg. Co.
16918 Edwards Rd.,
Cerritos, Calif. 90701

Index